TWENTIETH CENTURY INTERPRETATIONS
OF
LORD JIM

A Collection of Critical Essays

Edited by

ROBERT E. KUEHN

Prentice-Hall, Inc. *Englewood Cliffs, N. J.*

A SPECTRUM BOOK

Prentice-Hall International, Inc. (*London*)

Contents

Morton Dauwen Zabel   **112**

TWENTIETH CENTURY INTERPRETATIONS
OF

LORD JIM

Introduction

by Robert E. Kuehn

Unlike many novelists who draw upon the geography, customs and idiom of their native region for the creation of their art, Joseph Conrad's characteristic subject was not Poland but the sea, and he wrote neither in his native tongue nor in French, his second language, but in English, which he first started to speak around the age of twenty. His artistic career is singular and impressive. His first novel was published when he was nearly forty. When he died at sixty-seven he was the author of a long shelf of books; he had by then won both a modest popularity and the esteem of such literary men as Henry James and André Gide. His reputation, which faded for fifteen or twenty years after his death, is now very high and his work is the object of considerable critical inquiry. Critics continue to debate the meaning and importance of his work and, as this collection of essays demonstrates, even *Lord Jim,* his most widely read novel, enjoys nothing like a critical consensus.

Conrad was born December 3, 1857 near the town of Berdyczew in the Polish Ukraine, which was under Russian rule. His parents were cultivated gentry. Apollo Korzeniowski, Conrad's father, was a man of letters (he translated Shakespeare and Hugo into Polish), and an ardent Polish patriot. When he went to Warsaw in 1861 it was to edit a literary monthly and to help organize the National Central Committee, which sought the independence of Poland. For his patriotic zeal he was condemned to exile in a distant Russian province. Conrad and his mother accompanied him and both suffered greatly from the hardships of travel and privation. Conrad recovered, but his mother's health continued to deteriorate and she died in the spring of 1865. In 1868 Apollo was permitted to live in Lwów, Galicia, and later in Cracow. He was by this time seriously ill with tuberculosis and he died soon after, in Conrad's eleventh year. Conrad was from then on raised by his uncle, Tadeusz Bobrowski; he was educated by a tutor and later was enrolled in a Cracow gymnasium.

Conrad's boyhood was lonely, and it was no doubt to compensate for his own lack of freedom and adventure that he loved tales of the sea. His reading fed and strengthened his determination to become a sailor. His uncle, a prudent and methodical but kindly man, tried to dissuade him from such a risky career, but his efforts to encourage a less romantic profession were unsuccessful. In 1875 Conrad shipped out from Marseilles to Martinique on the *Mont-Blanc*. His shore life in Marseilles caused his uncle much concern, since the young sailor spent money freely and was perpetually in debt. Conrad's biographer, Jocelyn Baines, shows evidence that his gambling debts were at one time so great a source of anxiety that he attempted suicide; Conrad tried to cover this fact by pretending that he was wounded in a pistol duel. After four years in the French Merchant Service—years that were essentially aimless though filled with colorful incidents— Conrad shipped for the first time in 1878 on a British steamer, the *Mavis*, bound from Marseilles to Constantinople. He returned to England on the *Mavis* and in 1880 entered the British Merchant Service. In the next few years he passed successive examinations for third mate, mate, and master. He was naturalized as a British subject in 1886, and in 1888 received his first command, the *Otago*. Conrad made two very important decisions in 1889, although he could hardly have been aware of their importance at the time: he began writing his first novel, *Almayer's Folly*, and he made a voyage to the Belgian Congo. His trip up the Congo River on the *SS Roi des Belges*, which permanently undermined his health and filled him with moral revulsion, was recreated some ten years later with stunning detail in *Heart of Darkness*. He recovered slowly and returned to the sea for the last time in 1893.

Edward Garnett, who was a reader at the firm of T. Fisher Unwin, accepted *Almayer's Folly* for publication and urged Conrad, then nearly in middle age, to continue writing. *An Outcast of the Islands* was published in 1896, the same year in which Conrad married Jessie George and settled in Essex. In the years that followed, Conrad wrote at an exhausting pace—stories, novels, personal reminiscences, essays— and yet, as we know from his correspondence, writing caused him great anguish and he was rarely satisfied with what he wrote. His instinctive seriousness, his devotion to craft, along with a wavering faith in his own genius made Conrad's profession as writer an almost daily struggle. His fame grew slowly but he was acknowledged as a writer of the first rank long before he became popular. He was offered (but declined) a knighthood in 1924, the year of his death, and he is buried at Canterbury.

The authentic literary imagination is, with few exceptions, narrow. In the novels of Dickens, James, or Faulkner a characteristic pattern is repeated again and again. The variations upon the pattern may be richly diversified, but the pattern itself—which identifies the fictional world of each of these novelists—is simple, obsessive, timeless. By "pattern" I mean not a discreet aspect of fiction such as theme, character or even dramatic situation but a convergence of these which gives an artist his enduring subject. (I use the word "gives" since it is quite clear that the pattern is not consciously chosen.) Conrad is no exception to this rule. In the opening of his first novel, he describes Almayer as a man "absorbed in his dream of wealth and power away from this coast where he had dwelt for so many years, forgetting the bitterness of toil and strife in the vision of a great and splendid reward." He could almost as appropriately be describing Jim contemplating his new life in Patusan.

Almayer, Jim, Kurtz (*Heart of Darkness*), Charles Gould (*Nostromo*), Razumov (*Under Western Eyes*), Heyst (*Victory*) all have much in common with each other. They are all self-deluded exiles, estranged from their fellow mortals by a dream of special destiny. If the common pursuit of James's characters is self-knowledge, Conrad's characters are identified by their flight from it. Insight and wisdom elude them and by the ineluctable logic of tragedy they betray and even destroy those who have the greatest claim on their loyalty. Conrad was profoundly skeptical: the moral atmosphere of his art is harsh, and he sees little hope of the individual's reconciling his fate with the fate of his community or of his forsaking his illusions when they are clearly at odds with reality. Conrad's books *are* wonderfully varied, but self-delusion and betrayal is the steady center, the necessary obsession. from which the variations extend themselves. One can only conjecture that the pattern which stamps his art reflects some experience or fantasy of Conrad's own. In his biography of Conrad, Jocelyn Baines has speculated on this linkage of life and art:

> The idea of guilt or betrayal and atonement or justification dominated . Conrad's life. His leaving Poland was at the root of these feelings, although it is likely that his attempted suicide [in 1878—see Baines, pp. 53–54 for a full account] enhanced them. It is not stretching psychological probability to see Jim's "jump" or Razumov's "betrayal" of Haldin a, presumably unconscious, symbolical representation of Conrad's action in leaving Poland. It is particularly revealing that Conrad used the word "jump" with reference to his departure from Poland: "I verily believe mine was the only case of a boy of my nationality and antecedents taking a, so to speak, standing jump out of his racial surroundings and associations." (Conrad, *A Personal Record*, p. 121.) It is easy to see a psychological parallel between Jim's efforts to vindicate himself after his desertion of the *Patna* and Conrad's own life.[1]

---

[1] Jocelyn Baines, *Joseph Conrad: A Critical Biography* (London, 1960), pp. 254–55.

Eloise K. Hay, in her essay *"Lord Jim*: From Sketch to Novel,"
also reveals several interesting parallels between Conrad's own experience and *Lord Jim*. While the story of Jim undoubtedly had its
roots in Conrad's inner life, many of the details of the novel may be
clearly traced to other sources.[2] While sailing on the *Vidar* in 1887–88,
Conrad met a man named Jim Lingard. Lingard was a white trader
and he was known to many of the natives he traded with in the East
as "Tuan Jim." He seems to have been a colorful, swaggering figure,
but Conrad borrowed only his name, for his character and moral
history have nothing in common with Conrad's Jim. A far more important model for Jim was Augustine Podmore Williams,[3] who was
first mate aboard the notorious *Jeddah*. The *Jeddah* was an old
steamer which ran into a storm on a journey from Singapore to Jeddah (the port of Mecca) in the summer of 1880. She was carrying more
than nine hundred Mohammedan pilgrims. During the foul weather,
the ship, which was heavily insured, was abandoned by captain and
crew (the junior engineer, who was not quick enough to get into a
lifeboat, stayed aboard and was later made a local hero). The captain
reported the ship lost with all hands but, like the *Patna*, it was rescued
and towed to port. An inquiry followed and the captain's certificate
was cancelled. The craven desertion of the ship by its European crew
was reported in newspapers in Asia and Europe and the story was
well-known in Eastern ports for many years.

Jim's adventures in Patusan are based in part on Conrad's knowledge of James Brooke, an English adventurer who had had a fabulous
career and was the subject of a number of books which Conrad probably knew well. Brooke had come to Sarawak, on the west coast of
Borneo, in 1839 after an unsuccessful career in England and India. He
helped quell a local rebellion and was made Rajah of Sarawak in
1841. He devoted the rest of his life to his new people, but his career,
unlike Jim's, did not end in violent defeat. When he died in 1868, his
power was passed on to his nephew.

From these scattered sources, *Lord Jim* took shape by stages in
Conrad's mind, and the focus of the book was enlarged greatly as
Conrad worked at it. When he began the book in May 1898, he called
it "Jim, a Sketch," and conceived of it as a short tale describing only
the pilgrim ship episode.[4] The story was put aside several times for

---

[2] See Joseph D. Gordan, *Joseph Conrad—The Making of a Novelist* (Cambridge,
Mass., 1940), pp. 57–74.

[3] For a complete discussion of the similarities between Jim and Williams, see
Norman Sherry, *Conrad's Eastern World* (Cambridge, Mass., 1966), pp. 65–86.

[4] Mrs. Hay, in *"Lord Jim*: From Sketch to Novel," argues that (contrary to Conrad's statement in his Author's Note), Patusan was part of his original conception.

the writing of others ("Karain," "Youth," and "Heart of Darkness"), and for repeated attempts at *The Rescue,* which took many more years to complete. Conrad did not work steadily on *Jim* again until September 1899. The novel was finally completed in June 1900. It was published in monthly installments in *Blackwood's Magazine* from October 1899 to November 1900, and in book form on October 15, 1900. In spite of warm praise by Garnett, Galsworthy, and James, among others, and moderately enthusiastic reviews in England and America, the novel was initially unpopular. Conrad himself was deeply apprehensive about the novel, sensitive of its flaws, uncertain of its chance for survival.

Lord Jim is today Conrad's most widely appreciated novel and many also consider it his most characteristic work of art. Whatever the defects of this "free and wandering tale," in it Conrad brought to dramatic fulfillment his own most persistent and finally unanswerable questions about the nature of man. In its probing, oblique, resonant fashion the story of Jim, "a simple and sensitive character," does, as Conrad hoped it would, "colour the whole sentiment of existence." Jim is, as Marlow insists again and again, "one of us." In Marlow's unrelenting attempt to see Jim whole, to account for both his fine aspirations and his cowardice, to judge him fairly, we recognize our own difficulty in assessing character in the twentieth century. For Conrad as for us, there is no last word on man, and while we may yearn nostalgically for the unambiguous heroes of earlier cultures, it is in figures like Jim and Leopold Bloom and Thomas Sutpen, to take three extreme examples, that we discover our own authentic heroes and the "sentiment of existence" which is uniquely ours.

Much has been written about the structural weakness of *Lord Jim.* Conrad himself was uneasy about the division of the novel into the events surrounding the *Patna* episode and the later events in Patusan. In his letter to Garnett (reprinted in Part Two of this volume) he tells him he has put his finger on "the plague spot—the division of the book into two parts." And in his Author's Note, written sixteen years after the publication of *Lord Jim,* he alludes to those early reviewers who "maintained that the work starting as a short story had got beyond the writer's control." Some modern critics of the book, such as F. R. Leavis, support the judgment of the early reviewers.

While it may be true that the novel is too neatly halved (with Marlow's interview with Stein in Chapter XX bridging the two parts) neither half is conceivable without the other. *Lord Jim* as surely as any great novel has a single action which accommodates and gives significance to all its details. Conrad binds his tale with large and small parallels too numerous to mention but quite apparent to the attentive reader. However one interprets Jim's last acts (and they are interpreted quite differently by the critics whose essays follow) they are the final segment of an unbroken arc which begins with the training ship episode of Chapter I and ends with Jim's violent death in Chapter XLV. The shifting time sequence in the novel may obscure the fact that the plot of *Lord Jim* possesses an almost rigid inevitability and that the beginning clearly implies the end. Conrad's major theme—"the acute consciousness of lost honor"—requires for its full expression a deliberate ordering of deeply related acts. Jim's jump from the *Patna* is of course decisive in that it ends his career at sea, but I think we are meant to view it not as the climax of his life but as one of a series of unwaveringly consistent acts of character. While there is a radical change of scene and an enlargement of opportunities for the expression of his romantic fantasy in Patusan, Jim is essentially the same man in both halves of the novel. Although Conrad may initially have conceived of *Jim* as a short story (Joyce, lest we forget, at first conceived of *Ulysses* as a short story), his enlargement of the sketch into the novel as we have it seems entirely natural and appropriate, for the completion of Jim's character requires the Patusan experience. Whatever coherence, thoroughness, and magnitude the novel possesses would be diminished had Conrad not pushed beyond his original conception of the book.

When Conrad refers to *Lord Jim* as a "free and wandering tale," he is surely speaking ironically, for few novels are more carefully wrought than this. Incidents or characters which may seem irrelevant on a first reading only appear to be so. For when the novel is re-read (Professor Guerard is right in insisting that *Lord Jim* must be re-read), we discover that every character, every incident is a comment on Jim. The richness of the novel—our sense of its subject having been saturated with all possible meaning—is the result of Conrad's having included so much. Marlow's digressions, we discover, are not long-winded asides, for each throws still another light on Jim. And when we contemplate the man, we think of him not alone (as he too often thinks of himself) but in relation to all those others who give him scale and meaning: the *Patna* crew, Brierly, Chester, the French Lieutenant, Dain Waris, Cornelius, Brown. It is only by seeing him as a member of a community of men—some better, some worse than himself—that we are able to comprehend his moral condition. And just as the others throw light on Jim, he illuminates them, for in their response to him we read their character.

Although readers accustomed to the formal complexities of much

modern fiction may not find Conrad's method as puzzling as contemporary reviewers of the novel found it, we may still ask why Conrad did not tell his story in a more conventional way. Instead of a
linear rendering of events by an omniscient narrator, we have, beginning with Chapter V, a kind of sustained reverie in which Marlow
struggles to create an impression of Jim from personal observation,
from reports and assessments of him by others, and from prolonged
reflection and conjecture. The even flow of time is interrupted repeatedly as Marlow pauses and searches for the meaning of a detail
or breaks off altogether to recall an anecdote (such as the story of Bob
Stanton) or jumps ahead to anticipate an event which will be fully
described much later in his narrative. But however halting, dilatory,
and indirect Marlow's method may be, we discover in it an undeniable
parallel with reality, for we come to know Jim gradually, much as we
come to know men in real life, and like our knowledge of the men
we meet in life our knowledge of him remains fragmented and incomplete. Stubborn lovers of simplicity may still insist that Conrad
could have achieved this without Marlow; they may even applaud
Henry James's characterization of Marlow as "that preposterous
master mariner." But without Marlow—and not only Marlow the
recording consciousness but Marlow the mariner—the novel would be
greatly impoverished. For it is Marlow who interprets Jim to us, and
the burden of his interpretation as Conrad dramatizes it is the finest
thing in *Lord Jim*. Marlow is a man of the sea; his profession is his
life, and he takes justifiable pride in having trained many young
men like Jim for the profession. At the inquiry he is moved by the
pitiful sight of Jim and he is made profoundly uneasy by the moral
and philosophical questions raised by Jim's failure to behave honor-
ably under stress. At the very heart of his concern there exists the
nagging paradox of appearance and reality: "I would have trusted the
deck to that youngster on the strength of a single glance and gone to
sleep with both eyes—and, by Jove, it wouldn't have been safe."
(Chapter V) Jim jeopardizes Marlow's faith in the rules of the craft
and his faith in his ability to judge a man by his appearance. Jim
becomes Marlow's private obsession and Jim's longing to atone for
his betrayal becomes Marlow's frail and secret hope. If Jim's moment
of moral awakening is his jump from the *Patna*, Marlow's is his initial attachment to Jim. For the attachment forces Marlow into an
agony of speculation on human nature and its variance with fixed
standards of conduct, and his insistent telling of Jim's tale reminds
us of Coleridge's mariner, who had to share his terrible knowledge of
sin and redemption with others. Nowhere is Marlow's burden of
living with his knowledge more evident than in his reply to Jewel in

Chapter XXXIII: ". . . he is not good enough. . . . Nobody, nobody is good enough." What is for Jim an aberrant moment in his personal history, a disgrace which may somehow be eradicated in time, is for Marlow a permanent wound. Jim's impudent question—"Do you know what *you* would have done?"—is ignored by Marlow, but it is a question which must have forced itself upon him even if he does not articulate it. For Jim's fall has profound implications, and it is almost impossible to aviod self-doubt as one ponders it. Captain Brierly identifies his life with Jim's and the identification provokes his suicide, for he cannot live with the repellent possibility, however remote, of acting as Jim has acted. When Marlow asks himself "if the obscure truth involved were momentous enough to affect mankind's conception of itself," he is not giving in to mere rhetoric, he is hinting at the philosophical magnitude with which Jim's case may be viewed. Marlow lives with his obscure truth and he tries vainly to balance his tender pity for flesh with his grave conviction in the necessity of law. "Nobody, nobody is good enough": Marlow has come to view life as a mystery and a tragedy, he has drunk the cup and seen the spider. This tragic sense of life—so common in the great literature of the past and so uncommon in the bourgeois fiction of the nineteenth century— grows steadily in the novel, and its authenticity is the result of Conrad's method of narrating his story through a fully characterized intermediator.

The ability to see a paradox is a measure of intellectual worth, the ability to live with it a measure of a man's composure and fortitude. While Jim embodies a paradox, he lacks the insight to understand it. As a youth he fancies himself "always as an example of devotion to duty, and as unflinching as a hero in a book," yet he fails to respond during the storm aboard the training ship, and is contemptuous of the others who did. He learns nothing about his character from the incident; he rationalizes his behavior and so passes more deeply into self-deception. He goes to sea for the wrong reasons; its reward—the work itself—eludes him; and he is made chief mate of a ship

> without ever having been tested by those events of the sea that show in the light of day the inner worth of a man, the edge of his temper, and the fibre of his stuff; that reveal the quality of his resistance and the secret truth of his pretences, not only to others but also to himself. (Chapter II)

Before the test comes aboard the *Patna,* Jim is lamed by a falling spar during a storm. Lying low, out of the eye of others, "he felt secretly glad he had not to go on deck." As he heals in the hospital on shore, he is overcome by the "determination to lounge safely through existence." His intellectual simplicity allows him to believe in the possibility of a safe existence, and his self-esteem assures him that he is somehow different from other seamen who have been stranded in the East and have become drifters. It is in this mood and for these reasons that he signs on as chief mate of the *Patna*. The easy, undisciplined life on the *Patna* provides Jim with countless opportunities for self-congratulation as he compares himself to the other officers of the ship. This self-flattery would not have been possible in the competition of the home service which Jim has abandoned, and so isolated and confident is he that he fails to see that he is degraded by the company he keeps.

> The quality of these men did not matter; he rubbed shoulders with them, but they could not touch him; he shared the air they breathed, but he was different. . . . (Chapter III)

Our own vision of Jim is kept clear by Conrad, who narrates these crucial opening chapters and who reminds us that

> in our hearts we trust for our salvation in the men that surround us, in the sights that fill our eyes, in the sounds that fill our ears, and in the air that fills our lungs. . . . (Chapter III)

Jim is damned for joining the damned, and his decision to imitate their worthless way of life makes his jump from the *Patna* less surprising to us than it is to him: he has been in their boat all along. The grisly ritual in the life boat—"They had a drink from the waterbreaker and I drank, too"—confirms their community.

In "The Secret Sharer" (which should be read back-to-back with *Lord Jim*), Conrad's young captain asks himself: "I wondered how far I should turn out faithful to that ideal conception of one's own personality every man sets up for himself secretly." The Captain undergoes his trial successfully partly because he is capable of asking that question, because he sees that in every life a division exists between the ideal and the real self, and that in a life consecrated to action reality will sooner or later provide a test which will trace the congruity between the two. Jim is incapable of asking the question because he has no capacity for philosophical speculation; he becomes aware of the split between his ideal and real self only after his act of cowardice. Even after his disgrace, he says of his abandonment of the ship: "I had jumped. . . . It seems." *Seems* of course emphasizes Jim's inability quite to acknowledge the disparity between his will and his act. His jump is a fact which he has great difficulty in admitting. His contempt of facts is of course a contempt of reality, and his naïve disbelief in their relevance—at the inquiry he thinks, "They demanded facts from him, as if facts could explain anything!"—is a gauge of his innate resistance to truth.

If *Lord Jim* had ended at this point, we would have little more than a tale of the failed romantic will. These introductory chapters which precede Marlow's narrative give us a view of Jim which is ironic but uncomplicated. But with Marlow's appearance in Chapter V the irony becomes muted and discontinuous and our simple view of Jim gives way to Marlow's more complicated view of him. Marlow is puzzled first of all by the very different impression that Jim makes in comparison with the others from the *Patna* whose "persons somehow fitted the tale that was public property."

In Chapter VII the ambiguity on which the novel rests is expressed fully for the first time. To Marlow's experienced eye, Jim is an enigma:

> And all the time I had before me these blue, boyish eyes looking straight into mine, this young face, these capable shoulders, the open bronzed forehead with a white line under the roots of clustering fair hair, this appearance appealing at sight to all my sympathies: this frank aspect, the artless smile, the youthful seriousness. He was of the right sort; he was one of us. He talked soberly, with a sort of composed unreserve, and with a quiet bearing that might have been the outcome of manly self-control, of impudence, of callousness, a colossal unconsciousness, of a gigantic deception. Who can tell! . . . I listened [to him] with concentrated attention, not daring to stir in my chair; I wanted to know— and to this day I don't know. I can only guess. (Chapter VII)

Marlow sees through Jim's dodges and yet he insists that Jim *is* different from the others, for he does not try to minimize the significance of what he has done. But Marlow is nevertheless disappointed in Jim's failure quite to understand the meaning of his experience. For Jim is more concerned with the loss of acclaim which staying aboard the *Patna* would have brought him (Jim characteristically fails to catch Marlow's barbed witticism: "It is unfortunate you didn't know beforehand!") than he is with his betrayal of the pilgrims; he makes too much of his disgrace and too little of his guilt.

Chapters VII through XVII, which are set in the Malabar House and which record Marlow's several long conversations with Jim, are, in my view, the most successful in the novel. One would have to search earnestly to find anything finer in modern fiction. Conrad has perfect control of his material and he moves easily from one scene to another (almost everything that we remember vividly in *Lord Jim* is contained in these ten superb chapters), and the reader becomes increasingly and irresistibly implicated in the story as he identifies more and more closely with Marlow. The questions which trouble Marlow also trouble us, and our attitude is as restless as his; we feel compassion for Jim one moment and irritation with him the next. Throughout these wonderfully varied and modulated chapters we see and hear and feel with that heightened attention to detail and nuance which great dramatic art provokes. Marlow acts as ally and confessor to Jim, but even in these intensely intimate scenes the fundamental differences between his view of reality and Jim's are constant. Nowhere is this contrast made more explicit than in Chapter VII when Jim says, "I always thought that if a fellow could begin with a clean slate . . ." and Marlow, after Jim leaves his room, muses, "A clean slate, did he say? As if the initial word of each our destiny were not graven in imperishable characters upon the face of rock." At no point in the novel is Marlow's identification with Jim exact, for had it been Conrad would have relinquished that tension which constantly renews his subject. Marlow is drawn to Jim, but at the same time he remains loyal to that code of ethics which Jim's conduct has defied.

Jim gives up one job after another, always in flight from the exposure of his identity and his past, always in search of that opportunity to prove to himself and the world that he is better than—in fact the moral opposite of—the man who jumped. Marlow remains puzzled: "I could never make up my mind . . . whether his line of conduct amounted to shirking his ghost or facing it out." Marlow describes Jim to his friend Stein, and Stein understands Jim at once: "He is romantic—romantic. . . . And that is very bad—very bad. . . . Very good, too." He knows that Jim must be buried from the public eye and he effectively does this by making him his agent in Patusan. Stein is quite obviously meant to symbolize an ideal blend of human attributes—he is at once contemplative and a man of action—and to stand as a model of human conduct. In my opinion, he has far less authenticity than, say, the French lieutenant or Cornelius, and he is wheeled in and out of the novel in a rather solemn fashion. His importance has been greatly exaggerated by some critics, and his tortuously metaphorical prescription of "how to be" has been analyzed with desperate ingenuity in the hope, no doubt, that it would unlock the mysteries of *Lord Jim*. As far as I know, it has not. Stein's presence of course cannot be ignored, but, like all the characters in the novel, except Jim and Marlow, he is peripheral, a member of a chorus of figures who surround the two men whose shared experience is the real subject of the story.

Jim's early adventures in Patusan require little comment. In that remote land he acts out his fantasy of himself: he conquers his enemies, he earns the adoration of his people, and he wins the hand of a beautiful maiden. In his own eyes he is invincible, and reality seems at last to bestow its affirmation. But even before Brown invades Patusan and brings Jim's dream to an end, he is nearly slain. Careless of his safety, he sleeps as his would-be assassins plot to kill him. It is Jewel who has kept watch, who wakes him, and who orders him to defend himself against his assailants: "Fire! Defend yourself." He is still the preoccupied young sailor in the fore-top, and it is little wonder that so many others look out for him—Marlow, Stein, Jewel, Tamb' Itam—since he is so clearly unable to look out for himself. Cornelius calls him "a little child," and there is truth in this characterization. His disregard of Cornelius is an indication of his moral naïveté and vulnerability. He has too much confidence in himself, too much faith in benign circumstance, altogether too little sense of the evil in others. The man's wide experience of life has taught him almost nothing; his knowledge of himself and the world is a boy's. He collapses suddenly and completely when Brown arrives, for he fails utterly to sense the man's malignity. Instead of killing Brown and his men, who are trapped on a knoll above the creek, he goes to confront Brown as Cornelius predicted he would. Brown knows nothing about the *Patna* affair, but he insinuates that Jim is no better than himself and hints that a secret bond joins them. Jim's vanity is wounded by the comparison. Instead of fighting Brown, who is after all merely a heap of human rubbish, Jim gives him a clear road, partly no doubt because he sees Brown and his men as phantom doubles of the *Patna* crew. He acts like a gentleman when he should act ruthlessly, and those who put their trust in him suffer for his error. When others in the village oppose his decision, he remains firm, and of Brown he says, "Men act badly sometimes without being much worse than others." He responds humanely because unconsciously it is the kind of response he would like to evoke from the world for his own act of cowardice.

The ambush of Dain Waris's camp brings Jim's leadership and his life to an end. Even though he is still the greater power in Patusan, he will not fight. To himself he insists that "he was going to prove his power in another way and conquer the fatal destiny itself." He comes to Doramin unarmed, sends a "proud and unflinching glance" at the faces of the natives gathered in the hut, and offers his life.

His death like his life is open to various interpretations—is it a a suicide, a courageous gesture of atonement, a final flight from reality to a place where at last "nothing can touch him"? It is all of these of course: self-destructive, wasteful, and yet undeniably fine. His early success in Patusan counts for little, since he leaves the country in a worse condition than it was when he arrived. He betrays Stein and Jewel and Tamb' Itam and goes to his death in the egoistic belief that his sacrifice will atone for the death of Doramin's son. To the end he is faithful only to his dream of himself. But he *feels,* and however futile and "excessively romantic" his self-sacrifice may be, it is the act of a man with a conscience, just as his appearance at the inquiry was an act of conscience. He would not run then and he does not run now. He is deeply flawed—self-loving and self-forgiving, boyish, passive, much too fastidious for the world of combat. But these are defects of his nature and they must be weighed against his natural virtues: his essential decency and candor, his high spirits, his idealism, his harmlessness. Jim makes some ruinous errors—ruinous for himself and others—but he is entirely free of malice. Brown outwits him and outlives him, but only because he has the cunning and ferocity of a beast, and no ideal of conduct, no dream of the self inhibits or even mitigates his spectacular violence. Jim is both destroyed and redeemed by his dream, and he remains for us, as he does for Marlow, something of an enigma. But in the end his fantasies are far less enigmatic and less repellent than those of "Gentleman" Brown, who dreams not of glory but of fire and carnage. That, to paraphrase Henry James, may be the mystery within the mystery.

Lord Jim: From Sketch to Novel

by Eloise Knapp Hay

"Tuan Jim: A Sketch," Conrad's original version of the first two chapters of *Lord Jim,* has rested in Harvard's manuscript collection for almost forty-three years—since the year following Conrad's death, when Jessie Conrad, his widow, harassed by a long sequence of unhappy events in her family and nearly incapacitated by lameness and diabetes, felt compelled to let it go.

I call it a version, for it is certainly more than a draft of the opening chapters we know. The penciled manuscript fills twenty-eight pages (fourteen recto and fourteen verso) in a small notebook. It presents a fully suggestive account of Lord Jim's self-exile "from the haunts of white men," a flashback to his years in the English merchant service, the shipboard accident that landed him in the hospital of an Eastern port, and his decision while convalescing to leave the "harder conditions" of the home service for an easy berth aboard the *Patna.* The manuscript Chapter II ends roughly at the close of Chapter II in the finished novel, with Jim on watch on the rusty old ship, sailing monotonously toward the entrance of the Red Sea.

This beginning, which Conrad dropped completely although he used much of its thought and even many of its sentences in the novel he finally published in 1900, is apparently the start he referred to when he wrote [in his Author's Note]:

> my first thought was of a short story, concerned only with the pilgrim ship episode; nothing more. And that was a legitimate conception. After writing a few pages, however, I became for some reason discontented and I laid them aside for a time.

Although the "Tuan Jim" version of the novel's beginning has been

"Lord Jim: *From Sketch to Novel*" by *Eloise Knapp Hay.* From Comparative Literature, *XII (Fall, 1960), 289–309. Reprinted (with revisions by the author) by permission of the publisher and the author.*

available in print for several years,[1] there has been no published comment on the differences between this first draft and the final opening
of the novel, and on what these differences might suggest concerning
Conrad's original idea for the novel. Without indulging here in a
word-by-word comparison of the two versions, we may note one important addition Conrad made while writing for the serial publication
that began in October 1899.[2] The Harvard manuscript gives us nothing of Jim's tendency to cast himself in the role of a hero—a tendency
which, in the serial version as in all editions of the book, was already
fully developed in the first chapter, when Jim, as a boy aboard a training ship, met his first emergency situation, and failed in it.

The beginning of the Harvard manuscript is similar to the later
version in that it opens with a visual impression of Jim after "the
Intolerable drove him away from the haunts of white men." At this
point Jim is serving as water clerk to a ship's chandler in an Eastern
port—or various Eastern ports, to be exact. In the published version,
but not in the Harvard manuscript, the first chapter then gives us a
four-page flashback to Jim's boyhood, telling of his decision to go to
sea "after a course of light holiday literature," his apprenticeship
aboard a "training-ship for officers of the mercantile marine," and his
habit aboard ship of dreaming that he was "a man destined to shine in
the midst of dangers." The published first chapter alone concludes
with the account of a collision near the training ship during a gale,
the boys scrambling into a cutter, and one of the boys heroically
rescuing a man from the water. But Jim "stood still," paralyzed by the
confusion of the emergency, his imagination lost in his dreams, unable
to adjust to the immediate requirements of the situation. Then he
wakes up and feels cheated, also contemptuous of the hero of the
occasion: "The gale had ministered to a heroism as spurious as its own
pretence of terror."

Eight chapters later in the novel we learn that the same paralysis,
"a strange illusion of passiveness," came over him when the *Patna*
struck the submerged derelict. According to Marlow, who visualizes the

---

[1] *Conrad Zywy*, ed. Wit Tarnawski (London, 1957). The manuscript, transcribed
by Alexander Janta, is of course published in English, though the text of the book
is Polish.

[2] *Blackwood's Magazine*, CLXVI (1889), 441–59. The serial ran for fourteen numbers, ending in November 1900. Many minor changes were made after the serializa-
tion for the book. For a discussion of these and the difference between the English
and American editions, see John D. Gordan, *The Making of a Novelist*, Cambridge,
1940, pp. 150–73; and George Whiting, "Conrad's Revision of *Lord Jim*," *English
Journal* (College ed.), XXIII (1934), 824. In my essay I am concerned only with the
major changes between sketch and novel, which would hold true for all published
forms of the novel.

catastrophe of the *Patna* with sympathetic insight, Jim's paralysis was the result not of an inert mentality but of an overactive imagination: "you must remember he was a finished artist in that peculiar way, he was a gifted poor devil with the faculty of swift and forestalling vision. The sights it showed him had turned him into cold stone. . . ." Coleridge's diagnosis of Hamlet's disability fits Jim very well. Jim's mind is afflicted by the "morbid excess" of one faculty, which leads him in critical moments to lose the *"equilibrium* between the real and the imaginary worlds," as a result of which "the images of his fancy are far more vivid than his actual perceptions." [3]

The effect of adding the training ship episode in the novel is more than incidental. It gives us a quick insight into the nature of Jim's "tragic flaw," which is then further revealed in Chapter II. It illuminates, moreover, an aspect of Jim's fatal imagination that apparently had not occurred to Conrad when he was writing the sketch. Originally he had left the discussion of Jim's imagination until Chapter II. Another of Jim's attributes—his ability—was more or less the subject of the original Chapter I. (It is perhaps significant that in the original manuscript Conrad capitalized "Ability" in Chapter I and did not capitalize "imagination" in Chapter II. In the book "Ability" is capitalized in the first chapter and "Imagination" is also capitalized in the second.) Conrad's discussion of Jim's imagination in Chapter II of the sketch is very similar to his revised discussion of it in the same chapter of the novel, but in the original sketch we must rely on what we learn in Chapter II alone for our knowledge of Jim's early temperament.

In both "Tuan Jim" and the published novel we are told that, after Jim finished his training and went to sea, before he joined the *Patna*, there was only one occasion on which the "magic monotony . . . the prosaic severity" of the seaman's life had been interrupted for him by an emergency situation. In a storm so violent that his ship nearly foundered, a storm in which there appeared "on the face of facts a sinister violence of intention," he had been struck by a falling spar and consigned to his cabin for the rest of the voyage. When inactivity was thus forced upon him, his "faculty of swift and

---

[3] Samuel Taylor Coleridge, "Hamlet," *Complete Works,* ed. W. G. Shedd, New York, 1884, IV, 145. A sense of impending disaster, probably founded in childhood memories, seems to have been as ingrained in Conrad's temperament as it was in Lord Jim, who had had no such childhood experience. (Hence, perhaps, Conrad's inability to understand why Jim's sensitivities puzzled many of his English readers.) Conrad's early life, as seen through his uncle Tadeusz Bobrowski's letters particularly, makes us wonder to what extent his chronic drift toward reverie may have caused his fear of emergency situations—his fear aboard the *Vidar* that he would go blind like Captain Whalley, for instance—and to what extent his tendency to dreaming was itself caused by early experiences of disaster.

forestalling vision" atrophied. "Imagination, the enemy of men, the father of all terrors, unstimulated, sinks to rest in the dulness of exhausted emotion." This is the crucial psychological "event" of Chapter II in both versions.

At this point in the finished book, however, we realize that for Jim "imagination" has two striking features, has in fact a dual nature. On one side, so to speak, it carries him away from "reality" with images of his own possible heroic actions. On the other, when an emergency strikes, his imagination magnifies the horror beyond all grasp. Both aspects of this faculty working together rob him of the motor responses he needs in order to deal with experience. Because of the paralysis such an imagination forces upon him, he fails both aboard the *Patna* and later in Patusan, when the villainous Brown accidentally touches upon his old failure, reminding him of its tyrannous power over him and challenging him in effect to prove his mastery over it. Of course Jim remains its victim. Having pursued his dream of heroism and rehabilitation to a new land where he could begin anew, he has indeed driven his rival self to bay and won an illusory victory over it through action and the earned love of men who depend on him. But Brown revives the tyrannous faculty to its full force. If at this point Jim had another sinking ship to protect, he could have remained firm. He has conquered the part of his imagination that produces paralysis through fear, but he cannot learn how to keep it from distorting the objective requirements of the situation. Fidelity is now partly a matter of admitting the truth of Brown's insinuations, and he is so passionately conscious of his old guilt that he loses the power to judge Brown objectively.[4]

This time he does not desert the men whose lives depend on him, but he cannot take arms against the enemy. And this time no favoring fortune turns to save his dependents in his delinquency. They are massacred, and all Jim's work of years is obliterated in a bloody sacrifice. As he was man enough to accept the judgment due him while his fellow officers fled the trial of the *Patna* case, he now accepts the ultimate sentence for his ultimate crime. Weary of failure and yet disdainful of men who never shared his exalted vision, he goes out to meet his executioner. "He was overwhelmed by the inexplicable; he was overwhelmed by his own personality—the gift of that destiny which he had done his best to master."

Such is the history of Jim's *psychomachia* in the finished novel.

---

[4] For a different, or at least a deeper, analysis of this passage, see Gustav Morf, *The Polish Heritage of Joseph Conrad* (London, 1930), pp. 152–59; Thomas Moser, *Joseph Conrad: Achievement and Decline* (Cambridge, Mass., 1957), *passim;* and Albert J. Guerard, *Conrad the Novelist* (Cambridge, Mass., 1958), pp. 149–51.

In the original sketch, imagination of a kind was obviously to be the fatal "gift" that would force Jim to desert the *Patna*. The sketch gives us, furthermore, the clue (despite Conrad's remark that it concerned "only . . . the pilgrim ship episode") that, after leaving the sea for good, Jim would make his way to a Malayan village where he would be known as Tuan Jim. Knowing how Conrad worked in his first two novels and the unfinished *Rescue,* which must have been outlined in his mind at the time, we could safely predict that "Tuan Jim" already foreshadows that Jim's fatal flaw will be active to the end of the story, perhaps leading to his death (like Willems' failings in *An Outcast of the Islands*); or at least leading to the failure of his hopes (as the illusions of Almayer and of Tom Lingard had led to failure in *Almayer's Folly* and *The Rescue*).

What is missing from "Tuan Jim" is any mention of the dual nature of Jim's imagination. Here we are told, to be sure, that he is a youth of "exquisite sensibility," who has developed a "provoking and brutal stare" as a shield against all possible mention of the intolerable—his desertion of the *Patna*. But there is no reference to or suggestion of the quality of self-idealization which plays so prominent a part in the finished novel. Already in the sketch we learn that he will come to be called "Lord Jim," which in the finished novel is so appropriate to one who has from boyhood fancied himself destined to be a savior of men. But almost any white man in Malaya, as we know from Conrad's other novels, could be known as "Tuan." In the sketch we find one key sentence that could be interpreted to reflect Jim's inflated egoism: "he became chief mate of a fine ship without ever having been tested by those events of the sea that . . . reveal the quality of [a man's] resistance and the secret truth of his pretences, not only to others but also to himself." Again, however, this is not necessarily a suggestion of Jim's pretensions to heroism. We can recall that most of the main characters of the first two novels and *The Rescue* had "pretences," illusions about themselves that could not stand the test of events. They did not, however, like the fully developed Jim, indulge in grandiose visions.

The manuscript sketch carries the reader in twenty-eight pages up to the *Patna's* smooth voyage toward the entry of the Red Sea. Nothing significant is left out of the novel that was in the sketch, and nothing significant is added to the sketch to make the novel—except the incident aboard the training ship that reveals the duality of Jim's imagination, particularly with respect to his illusions of grandeur.

We do not need this episode to foresee, in the sketch, that Jim's imaginative faculty will be the determining force in his life. Although Chapter I of the sketch gives no idea of Jim's motives in going to sea, the beginning of Chapter II tells us that, after two years of training, "he went to sea, and entering into the regions so well known to his imagination, found them singularly barren of adventure." It appears that Jim went to sea very much as Conrad tells us in *A Personal Record* he went himself, in response to a mysterious appeal of "innocent adventure," [5] or at worst of "romantic folly." [6] Like Jim, Conrad had found the sea less glamorous in reality than in books, but, like Jim too, he had learned his lesson manfully and passed all examinations with distinction. No less autobiographical, in a way, is Jim's "air of overbearing watchfulness." It is quite in keeping with the typical, "unforgettable Englishman" in *A Personal Record* whose face revealed a "headlong exalted satisfaction." [7] Disabled by a falling spar, Jim "was secretly glad he had not to go on deck." But in the sketch Conrad immediately explains: "exhausted courage is the result of exhausted emotion, and in the motionless body imagination, this enemy of man and the father of all terror, rests in a slumber that resembles the peace of conscious resignation." And this, too, was straight from Conrad's life, as he later described the results of his own disablement after the same kind of accident:

> inexplicable periods of powerlessness, sudden accesses of mysterious pain; and the patient agreed fully with the regretful murmurs of his very attentive captain wishing that it had been a straightforward broken leg. Even the Dutch doctor . . . offered no scientific explanation. All he said was: "Ah, friend, you are young yet; it may be very serious for your whole life." [8]

In the manuscript Conrad struggled for over three pages to clarify his conception of Jim's imagination at the start. Apparently the state of Jim's courage bothered him especially, for he crossed out "exhausted courage is the result of exhausted emotion" and put "passive courage is easy since it is a sign that imagination . . . is asleep in a motionless body." Finally he crossed out the question of courage altogether, or perhaps deferred it, reducing the three pages to one sentence for the published novel: "The fear grows shadowy; and Imagination, the enemy of men, the father of all terrors, unstimulated sinks to rest in the dulness of exhausted emotion."

In the manuscript, curiously, Conrad seems as eager to excuse Jim's moral lapse in joining the *Patna,* rather than a home ship, as if the problem were his own. (The steamship *Vidar,* which Conrad joined

---

[5] *A Personal Record*, London, 1946, p. xiv.
[6] *Ibid.,* p. 43.
[7] *Ibid.,* p. 40.
[8] *The Mirror of the Sea,* London, 1946, pp. 54–55.

after his hospitalization in Singapore, was indeed an "Eastern ship," principally owned by an Arab.)[9] This would make sense if he did in fact begin by identifying the romantic youth with himself emotionally[10] while giving him the physical traits of a typical Englishman, according to his early idealized notion. The story originally contemplated was evidently a sort of *Hamlet* of the sea, with the difference that Jim's imaginative faculty would have forced him to two failures, one aboard the *Patna* and one in Patusan. As in *Hamlet*, the hero's imagination would have been the mark of his superiority as well as the cause of his undoing. Hamlet was no egoist, and neither was the original Jim. Jim was no less and no more than what we find him to be in Chapter II of both sketch and novel.

In both versions of this chapter the imagination that made Jim go to sea deserted him after he was crippled by a falling spar, during his first bad storm at sea. This is Jim's first emergency situation in the sketch, his second in the novel. And because this catastrophe, in the sketch, merely cripples him without testing his moral stamina, the atrophy of his imagination leads quite simply and logically to his decision to join the *Patna*. In the novel, when the element of self-idealization is added in the training-ship episode, the reader should feel Jim's surrender to the easy life of the Eastern seas as a second and more serious moral lapse. At this point in the sketch, one's attention is drawn rather to Jim's gradual, almost imperceptible regression from the weeks of his hospital life, through the period of his unsuccessful search for a home ship, to the easy job he takes aboard the *Patna*. And, in the sketch, Conrad had already provided Jim with a strong alibi immediately after the accident, making the failure of his mental powers a perfectly normal reaction of his physical disability:

[9] G. Jean-Aubry gives an account of the circumstances in which Conrad joined the *Vidar* in *La Vie de Conrad*, translated by Helen Sebba as *The Sea Dreamer*, New York, 1957, pp. 119–20.

[10] That Conrad was often arrested by accounts of actual villainies, which "sprang to life" for him when his mind sought extenuating circumstances for renegades who had committed them, is now commonly recognized. Lord Jim was based on one of the officers who abandoned an actual ship named the *Jeddah*. Nostromo has recently been traced by John Halverson and Ian Watt (*RES*, n.s., X, 1959, 45–52) to another unregenerate criminal. The originals of Gasper Ruiz and Razumov are other examples among Conrad's characters, to mention only two. The question of why Conrad manipulated characters in this way, however, is far more complex than has been fully explained. That he was sympathetic with anarchistic types is one suggestion, but this does not adequately explain why he made villains more villainous than the life, rather than heroes out of certain anarchistic figures. Kurtz in *Heart of Darkness* and Peter Ivanovitch in *Under Western Eyes* are good examples. Clearly Conrad had a more discerning consciousness of law and lawbreaking than would be indicated if his leaning were consistently toward lawlessness.

Imagination . . . must have something to feed upon, otherwise it sinks to rest. One admits the possibility of being struck from behind in sleep or in the dark, but one does not believe in it till the blow comes. It is otherwise when meeting the danger with brain, eye and hand.

The second and third sentences of this passage, and the imperative "must" of the first—Conrad's valid justification for Jim's apostasy— are missing in the finished novel, so that only a hint of the apology is allowed to remain. In the sketch, however, because of this justification, Jim's defense seems to grow stronger as his resolve weakens. While already in a state of mental flaccidity, he "had to go to the hospital. His recovery was slow and when the ship left he had to remain." Life in the hospital is languorous and makes a subtle appeal to his slumbering imagination, to his tendency to indulge in dreams without reference to mundane experience: "The gentle breeze entered from the wide windows" carrying "suggestions of endless dreams." Unaware of his condition, he is released from the hospital.

When he could walk without a stick he descended into the town to look for some chance to get home. Nothing offered at once and while waiting he associated naturally with the men of his calling belonging to the port. These were of two kinds. Some . . . had an undefaced energy. . . . Others were men who like himself[11] thrown there by some accident, became officers of country ships. They had the horror of the home service with its hard conditions. . . . would have served the devil had he made it only easy enough . . . and in their persons could be detected . . . the soft spot, the place of decay.

Because of the mental lassitude that has come over Jim in convalescence, he surrenders to the moral lassitude of the second sort. In the novel at this point we are less certain than we are in the sketch that Jim, in his right mind, would have resisted "an unconditional surrender to the charm of a loafing existence." But after he had "listened for days to the endless professional gossip of these men . . . some responsive chord in his nature was struck and he let himself go."

Thus in both sketch and novel, as to some extent in Conrad's life, a crippling accident forces Jim's fatal imagination to become detached from the objective necessities of life and, as a result, he falls prey to the seductions of an irresponsible crowd of men. In the finished novel, however, we are made to understand that the moral lapse lead-

---

[11] The sentence beginning "Others were men who like himself," etc. is less ambiguous in the final book than in the sketch, for in the book the tense of the final verb is "had become officers," making it clear that "like himself" applies only to Jim's being thrown by accident into the port. There is no suggestion that Jim is like them at the start in any other way, though he too did later become an officer of a country ship. He was not like the first type because he had not deliberately broken his ties with England to go East.

ing to betrayal of a trust was all the more tragic because it occurred
in a man who desperately wanted to prove himself heroic.

If it is true that Conrad changed his original conception of Jim's
psychology, adding the heroic "thrust" later on, there may have been
two very good reasons. First, he may have been troubled by a weakness in his original conception and therefore, as he says, put it aside
for a time. Second, something may have occurred to him—a new and
more ominous disability that could affect Jim's mind—sending Conrad back to the manuscript with fresh interest. Some such change in
thought seems implied when Conrad writes in the Author's Note to
Lord Jim that he suddenly "perceived that the pilgrim ship episode
was a good starting point for a free and wandering tale; that it was
an event, too, which could conceivably color the whole 'sentiment of
existence' in a simple and sensitive character." He goes on to say that
the original few pages "were not without their weight," but that "the
whole was rewritten deliberately," and that he knew the revised
version would be a long book, though not so long as it in fact became.

All this appears quite appropriate to the differences we have noted
between the first two chapters in the sketch and in the book, particularly when Conrad says that "the whole was deliberately rewritten,"
which is true only in the matter of conceptualizing Jim's imagination.
What is not so apparent and can only be a matter of guesswork is why
Conrad came only later to see the pilgrim episode as an event "which
could conceivably color the whole 'sentiment of existence' in a simple
and sensitive character."

In suggesting a possible answer, I must point out that it has long
been assumed without sufficient evidence that Conrad wrote the Harvard manuscript in the spring of 1898, when he first mentioned to
Garnett the stories he was planning to write for William Blackwood.[12]
Conrad tells us in the Author's Note just mentioned, however, that
the first pages of *Jim* had already been put aside in a drawer when
Blackwood "suggested I should give him something again."

A stronger argument against the notion that Conrad began "Tuan
Jim" in 1898 might be made from consideration of the notebook in
which he set down these two chapters. I have found myself looking
at the little leather notebook with its water-stained cover and imagin-
ing that it was among the keepsakes Conrad had among his posses-
sions, along with the half-finished manuscript of *Almayer's Folly*,
when his boat nearly capsized in the Congo rapids between Kinchassa
and Leopoldville in 1890.[13] It would be possible, even, to think that

---

[12] Undated letter to Edward Garnett, which Garnett places in May 1898. *Letters
from Joseph Conrad*, Indianapolis, 1928, pp. 137–38.

[13] *A Personal Record*, p. 14.

it was in the trunk carrying things he had on the Congo trip which Jessie Conrad says turned up unexpectedly in France on their honeymoon.[14] If so, possibly he took out the little book as early as that, in the summer of 1896, and wrote in it the first two chapters of "Tuan Jim," based on an actual sea disaster that had occurred in 1880. It is difficult to think why, if not then, Conrad would have used that heirloom, a commonplace book in which his maternal grandmother, Teofila Bobrowska,[15] had copied a number of Polish poems that took her fancy and made a landscape sketch in brown ink, as a present for her husband in 1819.

The book had undoubtedly been passed on to Conrad by his uncle Tadeusz Bobrowski, either in 1890 when Conrad visited him before going to the Congo or at Bobrowski's death in 1894. Conrad was in the habit of using full, standard or legal-size, sheets of paper for his manuscripts. The only sewn notebooks among his manuscripts are the two Congo diaries (also at Harvard and also written in pencil, but showing a handwriting decidedly more angular than "Tuan Jim") and the Polish commonplace book. All three notebooks were later scrupulously guarded by Jessie Conrad, apparently because of Conrad's penchant for destroying his manuscripts as soon as he was done with them.

Besides using the book for his first sketch of *Lord Jim,* Conrad made a brief note in it for a scene of *The Rescue.* It may be significant that this bit of *The Rescue* was penciled on the back of the last page of the "Tuan Jim" sketch. *The Rescue* fragment appears to be a note for Part III, Chapter V, of the novel, on which Conrad was working in June 1898,[16] and possibly later. As early as July 1896, however, and in France, he wrote to Garnett that he was "setting Beatrix [originally the name of Edith Travers], her husband and Linares (the Spanish gent) on their feet." [17] And, in the novel as conceived from the beginning, Part III was to be the section where these people would be first fully introduced.[18]

There are other notes on other pages of the little notebook following the "Tuan Jim" sketch which may be of interest to other scholars. What interests me here is only the possibility that Conrad carried the idea for *Lord Jim* in his head for at least two years before June 1898,

---

[14] Jessie Conrad, *Joseph Conrad and His Circle,* New York, 1934, pp. 32–34.

[15] G. Jean-Aubry, *The Sea Dreamer,* pp. 17, 47.

[16] Garnett, p. 139.

[17] *Ibid.,* p. 61.

[18] For a discussion of the original manuscript of *The Rescue,* see Thomas Moser, "The 'Rescuer' Manuscript: A Key to Conrad's Development—and Decline," *Harvard Library Bulletin,* X (1956), 325–55.

when he sent Blackwood's eighteen typescript pages of it—possibly
more or less a copy of the notebook sketch. That the rest of the "story"
did not come easily to him even then is apparent from the fact that
over a year later he had written only three chapters in all, and these
not even finished, when he informed Blackwood's in July 1899 that he
was sending thirty-one pages of *Jim*.[19]

This was by no means the first time that Blackwood had asked
him "again" for a story, but Conrad was under particular pressure
in July 1899 to complete the volume of which the finished "Youth"
and *Heart of Darkness* were to be a part. In February 1899 Conrad
was not yet sure that *Jim* would be long enough to complete such
a volume. He was still thinking, apparently, only of the pilgrim-ship
episode. By June, however, it seems evident, he had begun to see the
story as a long tale, falling into two parts—probably he had by then
decided to make Jim's life in Patusan as important as the events leading up to his desertion of the *Patna* and his trial. Patusan would balance *Patna* not only in length but in the very sounds of the names.
Conrad was delighted with the new plan, though he later had mis-
givings about it when he wrote Garnett, "You've put your finger on
the plague spot. The division of the book into two parts. . . ."

Whatever changed his mind about the tale between his writing of
the two chapters in "Tuan Jim" and his revision of these chapters
as they stand in the novel in all likelihood occurred between February
1899—when he wrote Blackwood he was not sure *Jim* would be long
enough to make a volume with "Youth" and *Heart of Darkness*—and
July 1899, when he knew the story would be novel length, "fully
40,000 words," presumably tracing "the 'sentiment of existence' in a
simple and sensitive character."

One event, that I will need to discuss more fully elsewhere, occurred
on February 4, 1899. This was the appearance in the London *Times*
of Rudyard Kipling's "The White Man's Burden," which C. E. Car-
rington believes had a vital effect on the U. S. Senate's decision two
days later "to take over the administration of the Philippines." [20] We
know Conrad's reaction to the United States' action, but we have to
read Chapter XXXVI of *Lord Jim*, where a certain "privileged man"
is entrusted to learn the end of Jim's story after Marlow has concluded

[19] It is unfortunate that neither this typescript of the first two chapters nor the
eighteen pages Conrad sent Blackwood's a year earlier seem to have survived. The
fragmentary typescript in the Rosenbach collection begins much later.

[20] *The Life of Rudyard Kipling* (New York: Doubleday & Company, Inc., 1955),
pp. 216–17. For Conrad's response to the Philippines episode, see E. K. Hay, *The
Political Novels of Joseph Conrad* (Chicago: University of Chicago Press, 1963), pp.
166–68.

his oral narrative, to discover how Conrad reacted to Kipling's attitude to the work white Englishmen were doing among dark "sullen peoples,/ Half-devil and half-child." Omitting for the moment the difference between Kipling's view of these peoples and Conrad's view of Doramin's people, we may focus on the difference Conrad immediately in 1899 found between Jim's view of his place in Patusan and Kipling's idea of the white man's burden. In fact, the "privileged reader" of Marlow's letter has expressed the main sentiments in Kipling's poem, as the chapter makes clear. Marlow's concern is to show him he was wrong "that 'giving your life up to them' (*them* meaning all of mankind with skins brown, yellow or black in colour) 'was like selling your soul to a brute' . . . only endurable and enduring when based on a firm conviction in the truth of ideas racially our own, in whose name are established the order, the morality of an ethical progress." After complimenting this reader on being just such an intrepid Englishman as Kipling would admire, Marlow finishes: "The point, however, is that of all mankind Jim had no dealings but with himself, and the question is whether at the last he had not confessed to a faith mightier than the laws of order and progress." Jim's last demonstration of keeping such a faith with the people of Patusan was one feature of his "sentiment of existence" that so lengthened his story after February, 1899.

Another circumstance occurred between February and July that affected Conrad strongly and may have left its mark upon the work that engaged him most during the period. In March 1899 a Polish critic and philosopher named Vincent Lutoslawski, who had been living in Boston and had visited Conrad in England, published an article mentioning Conrad in *Kraj* (The Country), a Polish journal published in St. Petersburg. The article, titled "The Emigration of Talents," defended the thesis that Poles, either living abroad or naturalized in foreign countries, were able to serve the cause of Poland as loyally as people who remained at home. "The work produced is Polish," Lutoslawski wrote, "even though it is published in a foreign language, for it is the fruit of the Polish spirit, differing from that of other nations." Lutoslawski said he could not "bring a charge of disaffection for their native country against those who could not remain in a suffocating atmosphere, who courageously went forth to take part in the universal struggle for the conquest of material or moral riches, a large part of which would be returned to their homeland." [21] Naming Conrad as an example of such émigrés, he quoted Conrad's words spoken during

---

[21] Joseph Ujejski, *Joseph Conrad,* tr. Pierre Duméril, Paris, 1939. I have translated from the French where this work is quoted. The original is in Polish.

their visit together in 1896: "I should never have dared to foist my attempts upon the beautiful literature of Poland." [22]

Lutsolawski's article brought forth an impassioned protest in the next issue of *Kraj* by a famous Polish woman, Eliza Orzeszkowa, who singled out Conrad's name among the émigrés Lutoslawski had mentioned because Conrad, like herself, was a novelist. Emotion carried her to assumptions far from true concerning Conrad's literary success in England at the time. She referred to him as "this gentleman, author of novels written in English which are all the rage and lucrative as one could wish." [23] With female precision she found her way to one of Conrad's most sensitive nerves. His inability to support his family by his pen was an embarrassment all the more acute because of his ingrained prejudice against money-making—a prejudice common among Polish nobles, who traditionally supported themselves from their lands, in professions, or by services to the state. Behind Orzeszkowa's words rang a clarion call to heroism, familiar to all Poles.

> Is this the way creative artists should associate in the exodus? Till now it was a question only of engineers, attorneys, and opera singers. And now they are ready to absolve writers! If it were a matter of chemistry or even philosophy [a jab at Lutoslawski], I might see certain reasons for editing them in foreign languages; but if it is a question of the novel, a fragment of creative effort, then I am involved. I know our commitments to the corps, *fort comme la mort,* and with all my strength I protest. Creative gifts are the floral crown, the crest of the tower, the very heart of the nation. And this flower, this crest, this heart, to see it torn from our nation and surrendered to the Anglo-Saxons, who lack nothing among the goods of this world, and for the lovely reason that they pay better! . . . And to top everything, this gentleman has to bear what name? That of his direct ancestor, perhaps, that Joseph Korzeniowski[24] whose novels made me shed my first tears and feel the first flames of noble ardor and virtuous resolutions. No little Polish girl will weep a generous tear or form a magnanimous resolution on the novels of Mr. Konrad Korzeniowski . . . but on reflection, this incident brings me only a moderate sadness, for I have faith in real creative genius and I do not suppose that ours ever wanted to respond to the call of a canteen woman or a salesgirl of the marketplace.[25]

We do not know that Conrad read the issues of *Kraj* in which his case was argued, though it would have been natural for Lutoslawski

[22] Jean-Aubry, p. 237.

[23] Ujejski, p. 16.

[24] This novelist and dramatist, who lived from 1791 to 1863, was not directly related to Conrad, according to his own account. He mentions this to Garnett the following year, as if the subject were fresh in his mind. Garnett, p. 165.

[25] Ujejski, pp. 16–17.

to send him a copy of at least the first. But it appears that Orzeszkowa wrote him a letter. He harbored the memory of it fifteen years later when in 1914 his cousin Angela Zagórska unwittingly suggested that he read one of Orzeszkowa's novels. "Don't bring me anything from that shrew. . . . She wrote me a letter once," he replied cryptically.[26]

His most direct answer to this woman was in Chapter II of *A Personal Record*. Most interesting for our consideration of the revisions of "Tuan Jim" are his words there concerning his own peculiar loyalty: "The inner voice may remain true enough in its secret counsel. The fidelity to a special tradition may last through the events of an unrelated existence, following faithfully too the traced way of an inexplicable impulse." Jim's apparent disloyalty to the special tradition of the English merchant service was no measure of the truth of his "inner voice." But only after Orzeszkowa's tirade did Conrad see that Jim's desertion of the *Patna* "could conceivably color [his] whole sentiment of existence"—for Jim, too, an "unrelated existence," unrelated not to Poland, but to England and the sea.

Since Conrad began *Lord Jim* before Orzeszkowa's attack, the novel certainly could not have been first conceived as an answer to her, as Jean-Aubry and Ujejski imply it was. Furthermore, a careful reading of the novel shows that Conrad's view of Jim was less, not more, sympathetic with Jim after Orzeszkowa's outburst than before it. As we have seen, the original "Tuan Jim" traced Jim's moral lapse aboard the *Patna* to nothing more reprehensible than an overactive imagination and the effects of immobilization after an accident. If Conrad had begun the novel by identifying Jim with himself, even to the extent of questioning how a sensitive and highly responsible man could desert a position of public trust, it is possible to suppose that the argument in *Kraj,* with its emotional references to "the Polish spirit," revived in Conrad a memory of his past that suggested another dimension for Jim's dilemma.

Lutoslawski's earnest concern with "the Polish spirit, differing from that of other nations," and how this spirit could be served even by those who had left Poland for good, struck a note that shook the nerves of many among the Polish intelligentsia, who had been nurtured on the idea that every Pole was an integral part of a sacred number, of a sacred body that must not be desecrated. This latter analogy had been carried to mystical heights by Poland's romantic poets, particularly Mickiewicz,[27] who likened the body of Poland and

[26] *Ibid.,* p. 18.

[27] For a discussion of Adam Mickiewicz's messianic revelation, derived from the mystic Towianski, see Wiktor Weintraub, *The Poetry of Adam Mickiewicz,* The Hague, 1954.

her members to the figure of Christ, the suffering servant. Even the
more worldly Polish patriots kept the faith that Poland was under-
going a period of privation in the nineteenth century which would
end in a glorious resurrection, but which must, for the present, be
borne heroically as a continuing proof of Poland's moral superiority
among the nations. The living members must be content to be momentarily forgotten, must not seek personal happiness, but must live only
for the resurrection of the whole. This idea and faith had become the
ruling passion of Conrad's father, especially after the death of his wife,
during his exile in Russia when he wrote an essay called *Poland and
Russia* and had it smuggled abroad for publication.[28]

Conrad's attitude toward this generative myth was evidently very
complex. "The spirit of the land, as becomes the ruler of great enterprises, is careless of innumerable lives. Woe to the stragglers! We exist
only in so far as we hang together." These words, in the mouth of the
English Marlow as he begins the story of Jim's life in Patusan (Chapter XXI), remind us that Marlow's pervading uncertainty about Jim's
very existence is certainly more Polish than English. But there is a
critical irony in Marlow's image of "the spirit of the land," a suggestion of resistance to this spirit.

We see something of Conrad's own resistance to his political heritage in the ambivalent description he gave Garnett of the fanatic
patriot who was his own father, "a man of great sensibilities; of exalted
and dreamy temperament; with a terrible gift of irony and of gloomy
disposition; withal of strong religious feeling degenerating after the
loss of his wife into mysticism touched with despair." [29] Something of
this man's character seems to have gone into the remodeling of Jim
when Conrad began his story again in 1899.

Apollo Korzeniowski, Conrad's father, was a complex man—a poet,
a satirical dramatist, and a translator of Shakespeare and French romantic poetry. Not a man of simple character like Jim, he was yet,
like Jim of the novel, a man who dreamed of saving people, the
people of Poland. And like the fully developed Jim, his actions had
the opposite effect from what he hoped. Korzeniowski and his wife
gave up their lives to free Poland, pinning their faith on the rebellion
of 1863, which Korzeniowski helped to foment, but which failed and
tore down with it many of the painful gains won by Poland in the
previous decades. Conrad's uncle Tadeusz Bobrowski commented dryly
on Korzeniowski's heroic sacrifice after his death, remarking that his

---

[28] Czeslaw Milosz, "Apollo Nalecz Korzeniowski," *Kultura* (Paris), Feb. 1956, p.
76. This article was translated for me from the Polish by Mrs. Walter Drzewieniecki.
[29] Garnett, p. 167.

dreams had betrayed him: "I assert only that in general poets, men of imagination and ideals, are not capable of clearly formulating the concrete postulates of existence." [30]

Korzeniowski was far from unique among Poles. The poet rebel was a revered figure among a people deprived of representative statesmen, who had a political voice only under fictive disguises. Like the more famous political exile and poet Adam Mickiewicz, Korzeniowski borrowed from religion and poetry romantic myths prognosticating the rebirth of Poland. Warning Conrad against any such fantasies, Bobrowski wrote:

> Our country, as Slowacki well says (although he himself was not free from the reproach), is the "peacock of the nations," which, in plain prose, means that we are a nation who consider ourselves great and misunderstood, the possessors of a greatness which others do not recognize and will never recognize. If individuals and nations would set duty before themselves as an aim, instead of grandiose ideals, the world would be a happier place. . . . I have taken the motto *"usque ad finem"* as my guide, the love of the duty which circumstances define.[31]

Bobrowski and other Polish historians, brooding on the fiasco of 1863, probed into the motives of its leaders, distrustful of their heroic devotion. Bobrowski wrote that, although Korzeniowski

> considered himself a sincere democrat (and others considered him as a "fanatic" and "red"), he had in him, as I often tried to persuade him, a hundred more times the aristocratic instinct than I had myself—I who never passed for a democrat.[32]

Recently Czeslaw Milosz has returned to the question of Korzeniowski's interest in "the people," apart from his own dream of their use. "It wasn't that Korzeniowski scorned the people, but he sought in it essentially a capacity for national élan." [33]

Under Bobrowski's careful schooling, Conrad resisted the powerful influence of his father's personality and ideas. There is every evidence that Korzeniowski, while deprecating his own qualities, sought to make Conrad in his image: "a good Pole," that is, a man (such as

---

[30] Milosz, p. 70.

[31] Jean-Aubry, *Joseph Conrad: Life and Letters,* New York, 1927, I, 148. Wiktor Weintraub has called my attention to Jean-Aubry's mistranslation of "peacock of the nations," a quotation from Slowacki which Jean-Aubry's translator recorded as " 'pan' of the nations." Cf. the Polish original of Bobrowski's letter, published by Jabikowska, "Listy Tadeuza Bobrowskiego do Conrada," *Kwartalnik Neofilologiczny,* III, 110–11.

[32] Milosz, p. 69.

[33] *Ibid.,* p. 70.

Orzeszkowa might have respected) who would sacrifice everything for a heroic dream, the dream of national liberation.

Korzeniowski died when Conrad was eleven years old. Bobrowski became Conrad's guardian and systematically set about curing him of his father's influence. He strove to make sure that Conrad's "inexplicable impulse" to go to sea should not turn into a "romantic folly." Perhaps aware that Conrad's overpowering urge to free himself of what even Orzeszkowa allowed might be "suffocating" associations, in a land representing nothing so much as a coffin where his loved ones were buried alive, Bobrowski was concerned that he should not transfer his father's self-idealizing fantasies to the life at sea, expansive as the plains of Poland but free, and possibly also a symbol of irresponsibility. As late as 1891, when Conrad was thirty-three, Bobrowski was warning him to be on his guard against the idealization of self and of Poland that he called "the defects of the House of Nalecz." And the following year again: "Your weakness comes from the Nalecz Korzeniowski. Your grandfather and uncle were always entertaining projects which had no validity except in their imaginations. . . . Your father was an idealistic dreamer." [34]

Bobrowski died in 1894. How deeply his words affected Conrad we know, not only from the reverence in which he held the memory of his uncle, to whom he dedicated his first novel, but also in the impression of Bobrowski's wisdom traceable in Conrad's life and work. The motto *usque ad finem* might be that of every Conrad hero, from his unimaginative men of duty like the captains Allistoun and MacWhirr to tragic dreamers like Charles Gould and the Russian Razumov. But here is the wonder: through the alchemy of his genius Conrad breathed fire into the ashes of old wisdom and found the romance and tragedy inherent in the dry cautions of his lawyer uncle's confirmed stoicism. *Usque ad finem* becomes in *Lord Jim* the blazon not of the "realists" who scorn Jim's dream but of the romantic Stein, who sanctions Jim's fidelity to his ego's ideal. "That was the way. To follow the dream, and again to follow the dream." Marlow, Jim's father confessor, finds relief in Stein's diagnosis. Jim's self-frustrating drive to serve heroically "in the ranks" [35] gives him the knowledge of his own humanity that few men can bear to have. Jim is able to "stick" to the end of his duty, even facing up to the worst and most unimaginable trick his own personality finally plays upon him. Brierly's "sham" was his inability to face this knowledge, which for him (though not for

---

[34] Jean-Aubry, *Life and Letters,* I, 146.

[35] A major point the novel makes is that Jim's "yearning . . . for his humble place in the ranks" does square with the last discovery that "of all mankind Jim had no dealings but with himself."

Jim) invalidated the code that held his life together. By implicit contrast, Marlow learns from Stein that the pain of Jim's self-knowledge is what gives him—and the code he longed to embody—an "imperishable reality."

When Conrad added to the sketch of "Tuan Jim" the halo and curse of Jim's romantic egoism, he introduced a theme which was, though few of his English readers recognized it, a matter of concern to all Poland, and perhaps through Poland to all Europe. Conrad knew that the Polish heroic idea was potentially deceptive though irresistibly seductive. Even Bobrowski, an admirable public servant who had spent his life resisting the Polish tendency to quixotic idealism, was not perfectly immune. While exhorting Conrad to take citizenship in any land where he could make a useful life for himself, Bobrowski had reminded him never to forget what he owed "to the nobility of the race"—meaning nation—to which he belonged and would always belong wherever else he placed his allegiance.[36] Clearly Conrad remembered. But the study of nobility became for him more than a question of how he represented Poland. It became an inquiry into man's power for loyalty and sacrifice to causes which are likely to shift deceptively between public and private goals.

One cannot measure, one can only suggest the extent to which Conrad's efforts to control illusions about himself and his "race" became in his fiction a voice struggling to censure sympathetic dreamers, the greatest of whom was Jim. We must not forget, at the same time, that this same struggle may have armed Conrad with his unambivalent insights into culture heroes like Kurtz in *Heart of Darkness*.

If the argument in *Kraj* about his own exemplification of the Polish spirit, recalling his father's ghost and the ghost of Polish romanticism, brought to his mind a new way of regarding Jim's fatal imagination, it is obvious that Conrad did not turn to defending Jim and indirectly himself. Jim plainly failed, and failed more disastrously as his motives became more heroic. But, between the early sketch and the finished novel, the simple Jim also grew into a superb and unforgettably tragic figure. Into the new draft came a new tension, a straining to express to uncomprehending readers, English perhaps more than Polish, the power and glory of Jim's self-defeating ideal. The narrator Marlow cannot resist him, but paradoxically identifies his own yearning for proof of the seaman's code (for belief in the power of an absolute and unchangeable standard of conduct) with Jim's determination to redeem his failure under the code. It was as if Jim "had been an individual in the forefront of his kind, as if the obscure truth involved were momentous enough to affect mankind's conception of itself."

[36] Jean-Aubry, *Life and Letters*, I, 59.

While half-despising his own liking for Jim, Marlow can find no one, even among seamen true to the code, who is true as Jim is true—in full knowledge of his capacity for unwitting betrayal. Jim's dream of heroism, egotistical as it may be, may also be—like the Polish "spirit" —the burning energy without which any fixed standard of conduct is a cold shell, or "a bit of ass's skin," as the realist Chester calls the English officer's certificate in *Lord Jim.*

There is good reason to suppose that Marlow rescued Conrad at a critical moment in the writing of *Lord Jim,* at the point where Conrad decided to shape Jim's character more rigorously by introducing the heroic obsession. At this point he would have wanted, perhaps needed, another character in whom he could pour the full measure of his ambivalence toward men who consider themselves larger than life size. Marlow is nowhere in evidence in the two chapters of "Tuan Jim." Of course, even in the novel he does not enter the picture until Chapter IV, which seems not to have been written until the summer of 1899. We may recall too that Conrad, in February 1899, was thinking of *Jim* as a story to finish the *Youth* volume, that he wrote *Heart of Darkness* as well as "Youth" with Marlow as narrator, and may have decided as early as the summer of 1898 (when he told Garnett the Congo story he had in mind to write) that Marlow could serve as a connecting link between "Youth," *Heart of Darkness,* and the story of Jim. In any case, when Jim's tale became so much more involved than it started out to be, Marlow was there to argue Jim's brief as both prosecutor and defense attorney.

The power of Conrad's feeling for Jim, as well as the force of his judgment against him, are the responses of a man mightily involved on two planes, one personal and one public, with the dynamics of good and evil. The evil in *Lord Jim* is one thing on the surface and another beneath our grasp. It is of course the evil of men who have no sense of loyalty to anything, like the villainous *Patna* officers and like Cornelius and Brown. Less recognizably perhaps, it is the evil of "realists" like Chester and Brierly (as oppressed to romanticists like Jim and Stein, characterized by their ability to persevere in spite of, possibly even *because of,* their knowledge of human frailty and suffering) , who think there is nothing to life but external facts. But there is evil also in the impulses we uncritically call "good," generous yearnings like Jim's heroic ideal, that may give life its whole meaning but may also destroy the very things it hopes to save. Insofar as one can take a moral stand on this hidden Lucifer, Conrad strove to take one in *Lord Jim* and achieved, I think, a remarkable if precarious balance.

The probable influence on the finished novel of Eliza Orzeszkowa's attack, and the general argument about the Polish spirit that was published in St. Petersburg, has been hardly mentioned by English-speaking critics. Conrad's devoted biographer Jean-Aubry (in *La Vie de Conrad*, 1947) was the first writer in a Western language to refer to it, probably taking his lead from the French translation in 1939 of Joseph Ujejski's *Joseph Conrad*, where the subject is treated in some detail. Both Ujejski and Jean-Aubry assumed that the novel was conceived as an answer to Orzeszkowa's charge of disloyalty, perhaps giving more weight than it deserved to Gustav Morf's "strong conviction, sprung from a psychological analysis of the novel" (and published in 1930) that *Lord Jim* "is more than a novel, it is a confession. As a confession of a man tortured by doubts and nightmarish fears it must be understood, if it is to be understood at all."

My own reading of *Lord Jim* has long disagreed with Morf's contention that the novel should be read as a confession, the expression of a guilt complex. Certainly I disagree with Morf's view that Jim is "not a Pole but simply a neurotic." Without seeing Jim as a Pole, I would argue that he personifies a spirit very like the Polish spirit in something like the way epic heroes personify their nations. Because Conrad's attitude toward his nation was more ambivalent and also more intensely personal than were the attitudes of Homer, Virgil, or even Mickiewicz toward their nations, we would expect his epic hero to be at once more vulnerable and less single-minded than theirs.

I think Conrad did feel the need to explain why he left Poland, but to feel the need to explain is not tantamount to feeling a conscious or unconscious conviction of guilt. If Conrad felt guilty about anything, it was, at least as much and perhaps more, about his congenital and chronic drift toward reverie, a curious compound of inner vision with outward inertia, that made him fear he could not fulfill his obligations wherever they happened to lie—aboard ship while he was at sea, at his desk when ashore. He was in fact, we know, guilty of delinquencies (though unintentional, like Jim's) through this failing. In *The Mirror of the Sea* he confesses delinquencies at sea. And later ashore, in August 1898, while "Tuan Jim" was on his desk, he wrote his publisher: "The worst of it is that while I am thus powerless to produce, my imagination is extremely active."

This was the tragic flaw he first conceived as the center of Jim's story. When Orzeszkowa published her attack, he was undoubtedly wounded to the core, but she unlocked his word hoard. Our wonder must be at the mysterious way in which he then transmuted the stuff of romanticism into the material he needed to make Jim's story a masterpiece. Jim started out to be a sort of English Conrad. He ended resembling an epic hero, as Marlow saw him: "like a figure set up on a pedestal to represent . . . the virtues of races that never grow old, that have emerged from the gloom. I don't know why he should always have appeared to me symbolic." The only "race" likely to claim Jim as its symbol in 1900 was the great lost Polish nation, which Conrad held in both love and fear—a nation Tadeusz Bobrowski had called "great and misunderstood, the possessors of a greatness which others do not recognize and will never recognize."

Guilt and Atonement in *Lord Jim*

by Jocelyn Baines

In Richard Curle's copy of *Lord Jim* Conrad wrote:

> When I began this story, which some people think my best (1915)—
> personally I don't—I formed the resolve to cram as much character
> and episode into it as it could hold. This explains its great length
> which the story itself does not justify.

Like most of Conrad's statements about his own work, this is mis-
leading. Conrad was never primarily concerned with character and
episode for their own sake, nor, for that matter, with telling a "tale."
In fact, the action hinges on a situation similar to that portrayed in
The Nigger of the "Narcissus": a threat to the solidarity of mankind.
In *Lord Jim* it is an act of cowardice by Jim. The ramshackle old
Patna is carrying a large number of pilgrims to their Holy Land.
During the voyage she strikes something below the surface which
holes her badly. The officers alone know of the disaster and they,
except for Jim, the chief mate, decide to abandon the ship secretly,
leaving the pilgrims to their fate. Jim takes no part in their frantic
efforts to launch a lifeboat but stands dazed, hating their cowardly
antics, resisting their attempts to make him join them, and waiting
for the *Patna* to sink. However, when the others are finally in the boat
and the *Patna* seems on the point of sinking Jim jumps to join them.
But the *Patna* does not sink and is towed to port by a French gunboat.

Conrad raises the significance of Jim's action to a metaphysical
level and in his portrayal of Jim's spiritual Odyssey explores the
theme of guilt and atonement. Every character and every incident is
subordinated to and intended to develop this theme. But it is so in-
tricately worked out that it is sometimes difficult to grasp the purport
of a remark or an episode. And, as in "Heart of Darkness," one may
be tempted to wonder whether even Conrad himself was always quite

clear as to what he was trying to say or, in this case, whether there was not some unresolved ambiguity in his own attitude to the events described.

Conrad had attempted nothing so ambitious, complex, or profound before; and he required a correspondingly complex method to enable him to achieve his aim. What Maupassant had called the "objective" method had proved adequate for the limited aim of the *Nigger* but in *Lord Jim* he was concerned primarily with subjective states of mind and with the analysis of motives. Like Henry James he was determined to extract the full emotional and moral significance of a situation. For James

> The person capable of feeling in the given case more than another of what is to be felt for it, and so serving in the highest degree to *record* it dramatically and objectively, is the only sort of person on whom we can count not to betray, to cheapen or, as we say, give away, the value and beauty of the thing.[1]

And,

> I never see the *leading* interest of any human hazard but in a consciousness (on the part of the moved and moving creature) subject to fine intensification and wide enlargement.[2]

But Conrad was not prepared to adopt James's method because the use of an exceptional person as the central character would restrict the application of what he had to say. Moreover, James's method entailed getting inside the central character and recording his thoughts and feelings by means of interior monologue or summary; and Conrad probably realised that his attempts at this had not been very successful in *Almayer's Folly* or *An Outcast*.

He therefore chose an average person for the central character. In the Author's Note, Conrad called Jim "a simple and sensitive character," while Marlow says that "he complicated matters by being so simple" and:

> He was outwardly so typical of that good, stupid kind we like to feel marching right and left of us in life, of the kind that is not disturbed by the vagaries of intelligence and the perversions of—of nerves, let us say.

Nor did his appearance really belie him. He had "imagination," but that is not so very exceptional, and, according to Stein, he was "romantic," again not an uncommon trait. He was one of those who instinc-

---

[1] Preface to *The Princess Casamassima* (New York Edition, 1913), pp. xii–xiii.
[2] *Ibid.*, p. xii.

tively react to the moral subtleties of a situation but, possessing only an average consciousness, is unable to express them.

Therefore, as an essential counterpart to Jim, Conrad used the device of Marlow. Hitherto, in "Youth" and "Heart of Darkness," Marlow had been used to record a situation in terms of his own sensations. His role was now, as a character in the book and as Conrad's mouthpiece, to probe, analyse, and comment on the states of mind of another. There was thus no need for the author to commit what was to Conrad the cardinal sin of breaking the illusion with the obtrusion of his own comments.

Marlow then was the chief device for developing the theme. But, in addition, Conrad used a number of characters and incidents as moral touchstones for Jim's situation. There is the apparently impeccable Brierly with his "Let him creep twenty feet underground" and his suicide; the French Lieutenant—"What life may be worth . . . when the honour is gone . . . I can offer no opinion"; the happy-go-lucky Chester—"What's all the to-do about? A bit of ass's skin," and the oracular Stein with his "He is romantic" and "In the destructive element immerse." These phrases recur often, like musical themes, and heighten and enrich the impact of the novel by bringing a multiple point of view to bear on the events.

In the *Nigger* the threat to the solidarity of mankind and to the efficacy of the "few very simple ideas" came from James Wait and Donkin. But by their nature these men could only be a limited threat because, being worthless scoundrels, they were outside the circle in which these ideas ruled. Jim, on the other hand, was an infinitely greater threat because he was inside the circle. The phrase "he was one of us" is stressed by Conrad in the Author's Note and constantly crops up in Marlow's narration; "He was too much like one of us not to be dangerous." Captain Allistoun, the other officers and Singleton had been impervious to Wait's blackmail and of course to Donkin. Marlow, on the other hand, felt that Jim's action threatened to undermine his own belief in the "solidarity of the craft" and "the sovereign power enthroned in a fixed standard of conduct." "I would have trusted the deck to that youngster," he said, "on the strength of a single glance . . . and, by Jove! it wouldn't have been safe. There are depths of horror in that thought."

Despite the fact that Jim was "one of us" his "jump" had associated him with a group of irredeemable reprobates, the other officers who had deserted the *Patna.* But he refused to accept this association and did his utmost to distinguish himself from them. "They all got out of it in one way or another, but it wouldn't do for me." And Marlow was delighted when the French lieutenant saw the distinction:

"And so that poor young man ran away along with the others," he said with grave tranquillity. . . . And suddenly I began to admire the discrimination of the man. He had made out the point at once: he did get hold of the only thing I cared about.

It was the attempt of the "others" to link him with them that most disturbed Jim. When they were in the boat after abandoning the *Patna*:

"They called out to me from aft," said Jim, "as though we had been chums together. I heard them. They were begging me to be sensible and drop that 'blooming piece of wood.' Why *would* I carry on so? They hadn't done me any harm—had they? There had been no harm—No harm!"

Then, after the inquiry, when Marlow had got Jim a position with a friend of his, the little second engineer of the *Patna* turned up:

"He made it a kind of confidential business between us. He was most damnably mysterious whenever I came over to the mill; he would wink at me in a respectful manner—as much as to say, 'We know what we know.' Infernally fawning and familiar—and that sort of thing."

Finally, and most disconcerting of all, the villainous Gentleman Brown unwittingly tore the scar from Jim's wound. He knew nothing of the *Patna* episode, but, trying to justify the shooting of one of the Bugis community, he asked Jim:

whether he himself—straight now—didn't understand that when "it came to saving one's life in the dark, one didn't care who else went—three, thirty, three hundred people. . . ." He asked Jim whether he had nothing fishy in his life to remember that he was so damnably hard upon a man trying to get out of a deadly hole by the first means that came to hand. . . . There ran through the rough talk a vein of subtle reference to their common blood, an assumption of common experience; a sickening suggestion of common guilt, of secret knowledge that was like a bond of their minds and of their hearts.

Throughout the book it is as if two opposing forces were battling for the possession of Jim's soul.

The crucial action itself, Jim's jump, is presented with consummate subtlety. It is shown to be disgraceful, yet, throughout, Jim retains a degree of probity, so that the jump calls up sorrow and pity rather than contempt. Then each stage in the action happens so inevitably that it is hard to blame Jim. He does not decide to jump; he discovers that he has jumped. "I had jumped . . . it seems." And it is impossible to answer with certainty the question which Jim several times asks Marlow: "What would you have done?" "Do you know what *you*

would have done?" Marlow never answers directly, but he chews over
Jim's situation:

> He was tempted to grip and shake the shoulder of the nearest lascar,
> but he didn't. Something held his arms down along his sides. He was not
> afraid—oh no! only he just couldn't—that's all. He was not afraid of
> death perhaps, but I'll tell you what, he was afraid of the emergency. His
> confounded imagination had evoked for him all the horrors of panic, the
> trampling rush, the pitiful screams, boats swamped—all the appalling
> incidents of a disaster at sea he had ever heard of. He might have been
> resigned to die but I suspect he wanted to die without added terrors,
> quietly, in a sort of peaceful trance. A certain readiness to perish is not
> so very rare, but it is seldom that you meet men whose souls, steeled in
> the impenetrable armour of resolution, are ready to fight a losing battle
> to the last, the desire of peace waxes stronger as hope declines, till at last
> it conquers the very desire of life. Which of us here has not observed
> this, or maybe experienced something of that feeling in his own person
> —this extreme weariness of emotions, the vanity of effort, the yearning
> for rest? Those striving with unreasonable forces know it well,—the ship-
> wrecked castaways in boats, wanderers lost in a desert, men battling
> against the unthinking might of nature, or the stupid brutality of crowds.

Yet, despite Jim's "conviction of innate blamelessness," he was to
blame, and the rest of the book is taken up with his attempts to deal
with his action whereby he comes to a gradual realisation of its significance and to the fulfilment of his destiny. At first his attitude is totally
negative. "I wished I could die. . . . There was no going back. It
was as if I had jumped into a well—into an everlasting deep hole."
Then, when a Court of Inquiry is to be held, Jim decides that he
must face the consequences of his action and attend instead of doing
a bunk like the other officers. Nonetheless, dining with Marlow while
the court is in session, he tries to exonerate himself: "It was their
doing as plainly as if they had reached up with a boat-hook and pulled
me over." "There was not the thickness of a sheet of paper between
the right and wrong of this affair." "How much more did you want?"
was Marlow's pitiless comment. Since his youth Jim had dreamed of
"valorous deeds" and, after an incident on a training ship when he
was "too late" for a rescue, he had consoled himself that "when all
men flinched, then—he felt sure—he alone would know how to deal
with the spurious menace of wind and seas." But when the test came
he was not ready: "It is all in being ready. I wasn't; not—not then.
I don't want to excuse myself; but I would like to explain . . ." he
pleaded.

By deciding to face the Court of Inquiry he has dissociated himself
from the others who can merely decamp because, being morally

atrophied, they have no problem except that of survival. But in taking the first step towards rehabilitation he outrages Captain Brierly, who is on the Court and thinks that Jim should have cleared out:

> "Can't he see that wretched skipper of his has cleared out? What does he expect to happen? Nothing can save him. He's done for. . . . Why eat all that dirt?"

If he can't clear out:

> "Well, then, let him creep twenty feet underground and stay there! By heavens! *I* would. . . .
>
> "This is a disgrace. We've got all kinds amongst us—some anointed scoundrels in the lot; but, hang it, we must preserve professional decency or we become no better than so many tinkers going about loose. We are trusted. Do you understand?—trusted! Frankly, I don't care a snap for all the pilgrims that ever came out of Asia, but a decent man would not have behaved like this to a full cargo of old rags in bales. We aren't an organised body of men, and the only thing that holds us together is just the name for that kind of decency. Such an affair destroys one's confidence. A man may go pretty near through his whole sea-life without any call to show a stiff upper lip. But when the call comes—Aha!—If I—"

Brierly himself is the centre of an important and enigmatical episode in the book. He has been an outstandingly successful and efficient seaman, respected, envied, but disliked for his conviction of superiority. Just after the Court of Inquiry he kills himself, having left his ship in meticulous order. The reason remains unknown. Marlow says he is in a position to know that it wasn't money, drink, or women and remarks to Brierly's old mate, Jones:

> "You may depend on it . . . it wasn't anything that would have disturbed much either of us two."

and Jones answers with "amazing profundity":

> "Ay, ay! neither you nor I, sir, had ever thought so much of ourselves."

The only hint Marlow can give is:

> If I understand anything of men, the matter was no doubt of the gravest import, one of those trifles that awaken ideas—start into life some thought with which a man unused to such a companionship finds it impossible to live.

This rather cryptic utterance is partially explained by another passage in which Marlow says:

> Hang ideas! They are tramps, vagabonds, knocking at the back-door of your mind, each taking a little of your substance, each taking away

some crumb of that belief in a few simple notions you must cling to if you want to live decently and would like to die easy!

Brierly's suicide stands as a comment on, and a possible alternative to, Jim's own conduct. But it is not an action of which Conrad approves and he implies that it is to be condemned because it is fundamentally egotistical.

Nor does he approve of Brierly's condemnation of Jim's decision to face the Court. Marlow says:

> I became positive in my mind that the inquiry was a severe punishment to that Jim, and that his facing it—practically of his own free will —was a redeeming feature in his abominable case.

After the Court has reached the inevitable decision and cancelled Jim's certificate Marlow decides that he will try to help Jim towards rehabilitation and gets him a job with an old friend of his, away from all who know of Jim's connection with the *Patna*. But Jim takes a negative view of his action and thinks in terms of escaping from it, of living it down or burying it. His last words to Marlow, on leaving for his new life, are:

> "I always thought that if a fellow could begin with a clean slate—"

whereas Marlow's comment to himself is:

> A clean slate, did he say? As if the initial word of each our destiny were not graven in imperishable characters upon the face of a rock.

Marlow has in fact already formulated the crucial question:

> The idea obtrudes itself that he made so much of his disgrace while it is the guilt alone that matters.

Because he concentrates on externals and is obsessed by the world's opinion of him—"a sort of sublimated, idealised selfishness" Marlow dubs it—he does a series of "bunks" from one job and one place to another as his past threatens to catch up with him. At last, in despair, Marlow consults his friend Stein: businessman, philosopher, entomologist, and, like Brierly, another of Conrad's touchstones. Stein diagnoses Jim's case:

> "I understand very well. He is romantic."

Man's failing, continues Stein, is that:

> "He wants to be a saint, and he wants to be a devil—and every time he shuts his eyes he sees himself as a very fine fellow—so fine as he can never be—In a dream— . . .
> "I tell you, my friend, it is not good for you to find you cannot make

your dream come true, for the reason that you not strong enough are, or not clever enough. . . ."

This recalls an earlier passage, where Jim day-dreams:

> At such times his thoughts would be full of valorous deeds: he loved these dreams and the success of his imaginary achievements. They were the best parts of life, its secret truth, its hidden reality. They had a gorgeous virility, the charm of vagueness, they passed before him with a heroic tread; they carried his soul away with them and made it drunk with the divine philtre of an unbounded confidence in itself. There was nothing he could not face.

Stein goes on:

> "A man that is born falls into a dream like a man who falls into the sea. If he tries to climb out into the air as inexperienced people endeavour to do, he drowns—*nicht wahr?*—No! I tell you! The way is to the destructive element submit yourself, and with the exertions of your hands and feet in the water make the deep, deep sea keep you up." [3]

Jim is romantic and that, says Stein, is "very bad—very bad——Very good, too." It is a burden but it is also the quality whereby a man can know himself and exist for others. Jim must be given the opportunity to realise his romantic ideal.

Stein therefore arranges that Jim shall be sent as his representative to an isolated trading-post in Patusan, a remote district of a native-ruled state. Jim had already hinted that he needed the opportunity to redeem himself in his own eyes and in the eyes of the world, and on his way to Patusan "his opportunity sat veiled by his side like an Eastern bride waiting to be uncovered by the hand of the master."

He took full advantage of his opportunity. By his courage, integrity and understanding Jim created a peaceful and flourishing community out of the chaotic, warring elements which he found at Patusan. He had gained their trust and respect and love. He could with justice boast to Marlow: "If you ask them who is brave—who is true—who is just—who is it they would trust with their lives?—they would say, Tuan Jim."

Marlow, who visited him at Patusan, had made up his mind that Jim "had at last mastered his fate. He had told me he was satisfied—nearly. This is going further than most of us dare." But he had not eliminated his past. Apparently no amount of achievement could counterbalance the one action, the jump. Surrounded by his success he turned on Marlow: "But all the same, you wouldn't like to have me aboard your own ship—hey?" And Marlow could not deny it.

---

[3] Conrad makes these passages more obscure than they need be by using "dream" in two different senses: first as an ideal image and then equated with life itself.

When he was parting from Marlow Jim again understood the limits of his achievement:

> "I have got back my confidence in myself—a good name—yet some-times I wish—No! I shall hold what I've got. Can't expect anything more." He flung his arm out towards the sea. "Not out there anyhow." He stamped his foot upon the sand. "This is my limit, because nothing less will do."

He realised that he could not send a message to the outside world. He shouted as Marlow was being rowed away: " 'Tell them—,' he began . . . 'No—nothing,' he said, and with a slight wave of his hand motioned the boat away."

Then Gentleman Brown and his blackguards arrived to threaten the world which Jim had built up.

It has been claimed that Jim was "mentally helpless" [4] before Brown and, because of a "paralysed identification," [5] was unable to disown him, thus bringing disaster on the community. Far from being mentally paralysed, Jim "had for the first time to affirm his will in the face of outspoken opposition" from the Bugis. He succeeded, and Marlow summed up: "In this simple form of assent to his will lies the whole gist of the situation; their creed, his truth; and the testimony to that faithfulness which made him in his own eyes the equal of the impeccable men who never fall out of the ranks." His actions were in no way affected by Brown's innuendos. Although he was being quixotically chivalrous in the eyes of Doramin and his Bugis community, he was by European standards right to let Brown and his men go; the offer of "a clear road or else a clear fight" expressed the conviction of an honourable, civilised man, and not mental paralysis. It was also an entirely sensible decision because he could not have foreseen that Brown would treacherously fall upon Dain Waris's party and murder them. But the appalling disaster irredeemably destroyed Jim's position with the community. "Everything was gone, and he who had been once unfaithful to his trust had lost again all men's confidence." It is again a typical piece of Conradian irony that this time he should have been blameless.

He now had three choices before him. He could flee or fight, either of which would have been approved by his faithful retainer, Tamb 'Itam, and by his girl, Jewel. "She cried 'Fight!' into his ear. She could not understand. There was nothing to fight for. He was going to prove

[4] Douglas Hewitt, *Conrad, A Reassessment* (Cambridge, 1952), p. 33.

[5] Albert J. Guerard, in *Conrad The Novelist* (Harvard and Oxford University Press, 1958), pp. 145 and 149, speaks of Jim's "crippling identification" and "paralysed identification" with Brown.

his power in another way and conquer the fatal destiny itself." When he had persuaded the Bugis chiefs to let Brown and his men go, Jim had pledged his life against the safety of the community, and so he chose the third course and delivered himself to Doramin knowing that Doramin would exact death as retribution for the death of his son, Dain Waris.

> Not in the wildest days of his boyish visions could he have seen the alluring shape of such an extraordinary success! For it may very well be that in the short moment of his last proud and unflinching glance, he had beheld the face of that opportunity which, like an Eastern bride, had come veiled to his side.
>
> But we can see him, an obscure conqueror of fame, tearing himself out of the arms of a jealous love at the sign, at the call of his exalted egoism. He goes away from a living woman to celebrate his pitiless wedding with a shadowy ideal of conduct. Is he satisfied—quite, now, I wonder? We ought to know. He is one of us—and have I not stood up once, like an evoked ghost, to answer for his eternal constancy?

Some critics have asserted that Jim's life ended in defeat but despite the reference to his "exalted egoism" which recalls Brierly's suicide there can be little doubt that Conrad approved of Jim's action. Conrad's "victories" and "successes" always had a taste of ashes and death in them and it would be wrong to interpret as condemnation the comment: "He goes away from a living woman to celebrate a pitiless wedding with a shadowy ideal of conduct." Conrad would never have disparaged such a "shadowy ideal of conduct," and the context with the reference to Jim's "eternal constancy" shows clear approval. There are two other comments of Marlow's to reinforce this:

> One wonders whether this was perhaps that supreme opportunity, that last and satisfying test for which I had always suspected him to be waiting, before he could frame a message to the impeccable world.

and

> I affirm he had achieved greatness.

It seems, indeed, that Jim had no acceptable alternative. The girl was not for him. As Marlow had said:

> You must touch your reward with clean hands, lest it turn to dead leaves, to thorns, in your grasp.

And constantly Conrad harps on Jim's fate and destiny. Marlow is commenting on the final scene:

> There is . . . a sort of profound and terrifying logic in it, as if it were our imagination alone that could set loose upon us the might of an over-

whelming destiny. . . . This astounding adventure . . . comes on as an unavoidable consequence. Something of the sort had to happen.

It is a strange theory that destiny should be reserved only for the elect, for those with imagination, but that seems to be Conrad's contention in *Lord Jim*. Nor is it a question of a person fulfilling his destiny. Fate and destiny are forces to be mastered and conquered. Cowardice in the face of the crucial test was contained in Jim's destiny; and only by conquering his destiny could he atone for his offence. An act of cowardice had to be expiated with the supreme act of courage, the deliberate going to meet certain death.

Lord Jim and the Loss of Eden

by Paul L. Wiley

The world of *Lord Jim* is the world of steam, of the *Patna* as well as of Brierly's crack Blue Star command, an age of new men as much as of new ships. Of this era Jim is a typical, if curious, product; and the "infernal alloy in his metal," a compound peculiar to modernity, is present also in larger quantity in the coarser metal of Almayer and Willems.

In this subtlest of all his studies in the abnormal, Conrad found in Marlow, who is both analyst and confessor, a more suitable means for dealing with his material than the method of dramatic allegory used in the Malayan novels or the visual analysis employed in "The Return." A raconteur, like Conrad himself,[1] Marlow imparts to the narrative a flexibility that "The Return" never achieves. But in two crucial episodes, at the height of Jim's trials on the *Patna* and at Patusan, Conrad relies upon the allegorical device to excellent effect.

The whole psychological groundwork of Jim's case has the color of a period, one in which Oscar Wilde, oddly resembling Jim to this extent, violated a moral code and afterwards refused to flee from a court sentence that left him an exile. The course of Jim's experience follows again the stages of isolation and finally total estrangement from organized mankind laid out for Conrad's earlier studies in failure. Had the story ended with his leap from the *Patna,* he would have remained only a more sensitive and well-meaning example of inner weakness which results in the double betrayal of the self and of other men. His flaw is, however, of graver consequence to an established community than that of either Almayer or Willems for the reason that he derives from the tradition of Allistoun and has been thoroughly trained for the craft of the sea. He might pass, in appearance, for one

"Lord Jim *and the Loss of Eden" (editor's title) by Paul L. Wiley. From* Conrad's Measure of Man *(Madison, Wis.: University of Wisconsin Press, 1954), pp. 50–60. Copyright by the Regents of the University of Wisconsin. Reprinted by permission of the publisher and the author.*

[1] See John D. Gordon, *Joseph Conrad: The Making of a Novelist* (Cambridge, Mass.: Harvard University Press, 1940), p. 15.

of the mates of the *Narcissus* but for a specter that shows through this fair exterior.

Jim also differs from the earlier victims of the wilderness in that his withdrawal from an ordered society is caused neither by greed nor by fraud but entirely by a temperamental aberration. In joining the *Patna* with its disreputable officers, he takes his first decisive step away from the sphere of normal activity mainly in the hope of avoiding exposure to the agony of sensations in an existence which had seemed to him unintelligent and brutal. Although Almayer and Willems are likewise vulnerable through the senses, Jim's overly acute sensitivity, resulting in unhealthy nerves, is inseparable from, and in a way contributes to, his power to form ideals and to discriminate with regard to matters of honor and duty. Fine and unfortunate, with the habit of living in a mental world of romantic adventure which exceeds the possibilities of the milieu in which he is placed, he resembles, more than any of the other early characters of Conrad, people like Madame Bovary or Frederic Moreau, who, in the novels of Flaubert, become creatures of fate through excessive imagination and deficient will.

Jim's personality baffles Marlow largely because it is not one but multiple; and despite the atmosphere of mystery which the narrator creates, it is not too difficult to see Jim as afflicted by that division between mind and will which Conrad had previously studied in the Malayan novels and in broader terms in *The Nigger.* Isolated from the control of his profession, Jim discovers aboard the *Patna* that he is both idealist and dupe of instinct; and he acquires this knowledge at the expense of self-betrayal and broken faith. The episode of his temptation and fall during the accident to the ship is the greatest passage of analysis in Conrad's earlier work, comparable in its disclosure of the sudden and total disintegration of the bond between mental and volitional activity to the more discursive account of Willems' surrender to the powers of evil in *An Outcast* but far superior in its mood of unbearable tension and in the skill exhibited by Conrad in handling the scene through a satisfactory balance of the devices of analysis and visual projection so as to solve expertly the technical problem of "The Return."

The circumstances leading to the abandonment of the *Patna* all contrive, in what seems to Marlow an aimless piece of devilry, to assail Jim at precisely those points where he is most vulnerable—in nerve and emotion—and, by bringing to light the breach within his nature, to reveal as well his deviation from the norm of act. The "burlesque disaster" comes to him as a complete surprise, a thing wholly outside the range of his previous experience, and hence more terrifying than the storms which drove him away from the customary routes of his profession. The incidents follow each other according to a perverse logic so that he is absorbed by a sequence of impressions as novel as those first conveyed to Willems in the solitude of the jungle. As these new sensations beat upon him, Jim undergoes his customary, but now intensified, agony of nerve culminating in the emotional exhaustion which infects his will. Marlow's comment that he was afraid not so much of death as of the emergency accurately defines his state of mind. His fear results not in the impulse to self-preservation but in the wish to die in order to avoid prolonging the emotional torment. It must, therefore, be regarded as a defect of overwrought nervous feeling which does not in any way impair his courage when he faces the court of inquiry.

As his downfall progresses on the one hand by means of this attack upon his senses, it is completed on the other through mental deception. His fatal gift of "forestalling vision," of living through an experience by thought in advance of actuality, is illustrated by the way in which his mind, stimulated by emotion, creates an illusion of total disaster from the incomplete evidence presented by sense. His predictive faculty operates consistently inasmuch as the observable facts support the assumption that the *Patna* is lost. Only the final link in the actual chain of circumstances, the survival of the ship, renders the logical process absurd; and it is on this point that the mind appears to conspire with the diabolical scheme of chance to work Jim's undoing. This is the most telling example in the early Conrad of the plight of the solitary consciousness in a world not amenable to reason, of the mind in servitude to emotion and accident. The unconscious Singleton would have automatically performed the saving act of propping a bulkhead, which would have altered the balance in favor of heroism rather than cowardice.

Unable to withstand this turmoil of thought and emotion, Jim's will breaks. Yielding to the promptings of instinct, he takes to flight. One of Conrad's most brilliant strokes in psychological dramatization is his portrayal here of the life-boat incident with the elephantine skipper and the other officers of the *Patna* struggling frantically to save their skins. The ultimate temptation on the brink of the abyss, like one of Saint Anthony's visions of evil, presents itself to Jim incarnate in these grotesque figures, Conrad's principal caricatures after Wait and Donkin in *The Nigger*. For all of his disgust Jim looks on with a kind of fascination, as Marlow points out:

> "He hadn't lost a single movement of that comic business. 'I loathed them. I hated them. I had to look at all that,' he said without emphasis, turning upon me a sombrely watchful glance. 'Was ever there any one so shamefully tried!' "

In these creatures of the wilderness Jim beholds the animal instincts that have been his familiars from the moment of his signing on with the pilgrim ship, and his ignorance of the dark side of his own nature reveals itself in his comment to Marlow on the difference between himself and these other outcasts. By leaping into the boat with them, he cancels this difference, as Marlow knows.

The *Patna* affair as a whole, in opposing so sharply Jim's mental world of heroic ideals and the outer world of illogicality and accident, is a more complicated variation of the theme in the Malayan novels of the collapse of an artificial paradise in the midst of fallen nature. The imaginary realm, timeless and ordered, in which Jim dreams of himself as a hero and a savior contains values and fine judgments on the score of conduct which stem from a chivalric and religious tradition, perhaps the vestiges of that faith in Providence which his parson father upholds in a lukewarm manner. He wants specifically to be a Christian hero, to give his life for others if need be; and the irony of his story, like that of Lingard's effort to restore Eden on a basis of savagery, lies in the fact that this attempt to transcend the brutality of existence involves him ever more deeply in the toils of a universe offering no support for such a dream. In the *Patna* half of the story, with its exposure of all of Jim's limitations, the contrast between his desire to save others and his actual abandonment of the passengers in their distress is implicit in the action; but the Patusan episode makes thoroughly plain the gulf between the ideals that he has inherited from a civilized background and the rule of survival which functions in his barbaric surroundings. When he leaves for Patusan, he becomes, in the eyes of Marlow, a hermit figure:

> "It was impossible to be angry with him: I could not help a smile, and told him that in the old days people who went on like this were on the way of becoming hermits in a wilderness. 'Hermits be hanged!' he commented with engaging impulsiveness. Of course he didn't mind a wilderness. . . ."

Except for important modifications in atmosphere Patusan, enclosed by its wall of forest, borrows its distinctive features from the wilderness of the Malayan novels. But although the reader may approach this region of crepuscular light and silently falling darkness through the stories that precede *Lord Jim*, it is evident that the wilderness image has undergone changes relating it more closely to the almost surrealistic landscape of "Heart of Darkness" than to the fecund jungle of *Almayer's Folly*. The obvious difference in atmosphere between the *Patna* and the Patusan halves of the novel contributes to the impression that the story breaks into two parts, a division that Conrad himself admitted was the plague spot in the book. But the concept of

division does not seem to describe so accurately the relation between
the parts, which are not really segments of one cloth, as the idea that
with the opening of the Patusan narrative the key of the story is
abruptly transposed from that of psychological realism to allegory.
The *Patna* chapters form a necessary prelude to a more universal
theme, just as the analysis of Jim's inner cleavage on the ship must
precede a full understanding of his ultimate disaster. Although the
Jim of the *Patna* stands as an example of a failure peculiar to modern
life, the Lord Jim of the Patusan adventure becomes a more portentous
figure. Symbolic for Marlow of races that have emerged from the
gloom, he is likewise a symbol of man in the shadow of a gathering
darkness:

> "He dominated the forest, the secular gloom, the old mankind. He was
> like a figure set up on a pedestal, to represent in his persistent youth
> the power, and perhaps the virtues, of races that never grow old, that
> have emerged from the gloom. I don't know why he should always have
> appeared to me symbolic."

The great scene between Marlow and Stein in Chapter XX which
turns on the high theme of man's imperfection and tragic destiny provides the appropriate transition to events on a more exalted plane.

Cut off by the court verdict and his own scruples from the traditions
of organized society, Jim seeks refuge in a world without tradition, a
land without a past; and his initial success as builder and governor
represents the accomplishment possible to man working unaided in
primitive circumstances. Conrad lays exceptional stress not only upon
Jim's isolated state and upon the fact that his word alone is truth
but also upon the "secular" quality of his surroundings. The idea of
the Fall thus emerges strongly in this section of the novel and accom-
panies the motif of limitation very much as in *An Outcast*. Jim's defeat is, however, made to seem more ominous for mankind at large
than that of Lingard at Sambir for the reason that Jim, in addition
to being "one of us," exemplifies the fate in store for man in the event
of a breakdown of the bond uniting a community against chaos. Amid
conditions where neither the law nor the beliefs of European society
prevail, Jim gains at last his opportunity to play the role of Christian
hero and savior; and he becomes, like Lingard, the virtual ruler of a
petty state, raises single-handed an edifice based on fallen nature, and
finds himself endowed with a legend of unfailing victory and supernatural power. Furthermore, just as Lingard takes a central part in a
parody of divine judgment, so also Jim at Patusan appears a kind of
Lohengrin figure in fragmentary glimpses of a salvation myth behind
the mythical-religious allusions scattered throughout this section of the
novel. He descends on the court of Patusan as though from the clouds,

takes the death of Dain Waris upon his head, and dies while heaven
and earth tremble with unnatural omens which Marlow describes as
though they were the epilogue to a crucifixion:

> "The sky over Patusan was blood-red, immense, streaming like an open
> vein. An enormous sun nestled crimson amongst the tree-tops, and the
> forest below had a black and forbidding face.
>
> "Tamb' Itam tells me that on that evening the aspect of the heavens
> was angry and frightful. I may well believe it, for I know that on that
> very day a cyclone passed within sixty miles of the coast, though there
> was hardly more than a languid stir of air in the place."

Not, however, until the arrival of the marauder, Brown, compels
Jim to deliver a judgment which affects the safety of his wilderness
kingdom does the full irony of his assumption of the savior's role in a
fallen world become apparent; and this incident may be compared with
Lingard's vain attempt to judge Willems and contrasted with Allistoun's severity towards Wait. Jim's decision to let Brown escape is, in
the first place, wholly characteristic of the temperament of Conrad's
hero as revealed in the *Patna* affair, the fatal gift of a personality that
he tries and fails to master. Through his disgrace on the *Patna* he has
acquired knowledge of his divided potentialities for idealism and for
submission to instinct. But the flaw in his nature remains, and the
measure of self-conquest which he acquires at Patusan gives him only
a respite from the specter of his weakness and the memory of his guilt.
The surprise encounter with Brown, whose mad and ferocious vanity
is the counterpart of Jim's refined egotism, places him, therefore, in
the position of the hermit assailed by the evil which he has tried to
reject. Being likewise a social outcast and a leader, Brown bears a
grotesque resemblance to Jim; and their meeting may be compared
with the lifeboat scene on the *Patna* as the second notable example in
the book of Conrad's dramatic and visual rendering of a psychological
issue.

Brown's trickery succeeds because Jim, a fallible human and not the
supernatural being of his legend, cannot destroy his past even in a
land without a past. His faulty judgment illustrates not only the limitation of power in man that Conrad had demonstrated before in *An Outcast* but also the failure of an individual decree without the support
of a general belief or tradition like that which sustained Allistoun in
his contest with Wait. Jim deals with Brown, like Lingard with
Willems, in accordance with a personal creed recognized by the society
from which he has broken but having no relevance to the immediate
needs of a secular community for self-preservation. Faithful to this
detached ideal, he permits the ordered world that he has built to fall

in ruins; and this fidelity makes the sacrifice of his own life both chivalrous and futile.

The strength of *Lord Jim* derives largely, therefore, from Conrad's facing of an issue which takes form in the earlier tales but which gains ultimate expression only perhaps in the nocturnal panorama of "Heart of Darkness." The crisis underlies Marlow's brooding over a question which seems to him to affect mankind's conception of itself. His interest in Jim extends to the larger problem of the application of a fixed standard of conduct to the individual in every circumstance; for the fact that the standard does not hold for Jim in his supreme test on the *Patna* casts doubt upon its validity. The scene between Marlow and the French lieutenant has always been praised; and a main reason why it grips the reader is that here Marlow presses to the utmost, and without positive results, his query as to whether such a standard can be effective at all when a man, in a case like Jim's, is beyond the check of common opinion. To operate successfully, the rule should enable the conflicting elements in the individual to work harmoniously to the end of purposive action; and its failure to do so for Jim on the *Patna* indicates that, when the division is absolute, man falls away from the control of the community. The one remaining safeguard is, then, perhaps a simple eye for danger like that of Singleton or of the native youth, Dain Waris, in *Lord Jim* who sees at once the evil of Brown which deceives and betrays the visionary Jim. After *Lord Jim,* at any rate, characters who have this primitive eye for fact without the benefit of adequate mental resources appear more frequently in Conrad's early work.

Butterflies and Beetles—Conrad's Two Truths

by Tony Tanner

In *Lord Jim* when the sagacious and tentative Marlow recalls taking Jim's case to the wise merchant Stein he tells his patient listeners that he considered Stein "an eminently suitable person to receive my confidences about Jim's difficulties"; he also tells them, in almost the same breath, of Stein's curious private interest in beetles and butterflies. For Stein is a "learned collector." "His collection of Buprestidae and Longicorns—beetles all—horrible miniature monsters, looking malevolent in death and immobility, and his cabinet of butterflies, beautiful and hovering under the glass of cases of lifeless wings, had spread his fame far over the earth."

We feel, from the start of that crucial interview, a connection between Stein's distinction as a collector and his suitability to appraise Jim, to help him. And of course what we learn is that Stein seems to have an uncanny knowledge of the qualitative extremes of humanity: man as butterfly, man as beetle, he knows them both. Considering that this is an early book the suggestive hints that Conrad weaves into the scene work with an unusually silent and effective tact. Consider, for instance, the way the insects are differently housed. "Narrow shelves filled with dark boxes of uniform shape and colour ran round the walls, not from floor to ceiling, but in a sombre belt about four feet broad. Catacombs of beetles." Not a hierarchy of beetles but a great thick belt of them: and that last short sentence makes just the right sinister impact. "The glass cases containing the collection of butterflies were ranged in three long rows upon slender-legged little tables." It is those slender legs we see—clean, fragile, graceful, and artistic: the appropriate furniture to set off a display of butterflies. The analogy between Jim and the butterflies is pressed still firmer

"*Butterflies and Beetles—Conrad's Two Truths*" by Tony Tanner. *From* Chicago Review, *XVI, No. 1 (Winter–Spring 1963), pp. 123–40. Copyright © 1963 by* Chicago Review. *Reprinted by permission of the publisher.*

before Marlow has even broached the subject. "I was very anxious, but I respected the intense, almost passionate, absorption with which he looked at a butterfly, as though on the bronze sheen of these frail wings, in the white tracings, in the gorgeous markings, he could see other things, an image of something as perishable and defying destruction as these delicate and lifeless tissues displaying a splendour unmarred by death." While Marlow is *thinking* about Jim, Stein is *examining* a butterfly with great care: we feel that the very quality of reverent attention with which Stein studies his insects somehow qualifies him to make a key assessment of Jim. For the whole inquiry of the book is directed at ascertaining whether there is contained within the perishable "gorgeous markings" of Jim something, some quality, some essence, which will defy destruction, some "splendour" which will remain "unmarred by death." But Conrad is not so simple as to offer a one-to-one correlation between Jim and the butterfly: just as the analogy threatens to become obvious Conrad breaks it:

> " 'To tell you the truth, Stein,' I said with an effort that surprised me, 'I came here to describe a specimen . . .'
> 'Butterfly?' he asked, with an unbelieving and humorous eagerness.
> 'Nothing so perfect,' I answered, feeling suddenly dispirited with all sorts of doubts. 'A man.' "

Leaving the rest of that discussion let us re-examine Jim—bearing in mind the possible metaphor of the butterfly, a creature of beauty, a creature with wings which can carry it above the mere dead level of an earth which beetles crudely hug. Straight away we recall Jim's aversion to dirt. When we first meet him he is "spotlessly neat" and "apparelled in immaculate white from shoes to hat" and this fastidious, scrupulous dazzling whiteness is invested with a slightly mystical quality. For instance when Jim is received by the treacherous Rajah Allang in Patusan, Conrad first of all establishes the fact that the people who have gathered to witness his first appearance among them are "dirty with ashes and mud-stains." By contrast Jim glows with an almost supernatural brightness:

> In the midst of these dark-faced men, his stalwart figure in white apparel, the gleaming clusters of his fair hair, seemed to catch all the sunshine that trickled through the cracks in the closed shutters of that dim hall, with its walls of mats and a roof of thatch. He appeared like a creature not only of another kind but of another essence.

This is not racism, not a belief in white-supremacy peeping through. Jim shows up against the world. Thus when Marlow sees him for the last time:

> He was white from head to foot, and remained persistently visible with

the stronghold of the night at his back. . . . For me that white figure in the stillness of coast and sea seemed to stand at the heart of a vast enigma. The twilight was ebbing fast from the sky above his head, the strip of sand had sunk already under his feet, he himself appeared no bigger than a child—then only a speck, a tiny white speck that seemed to catch all the light left in a darkened world. . . . And, suddenly, I lost him. . . .

It is perhaps too easily portentous: the enigma could be anything and the encroaching darkness which finally seems to snuff him out is a touch of cosmic melodrama in the Manichean vein—but the intention is clear. Jim is a creature of "light" threatened by the forces of darkness; he is the creature of purity who stands above the dirty crowd. Throughout the book his characteristic stance is a superior contemplation of a life which goes about its muddled business far below him. As a boy at the marine school he was "very smart aloft. His station was in the fore-top, and often from there he looked down, with the contempt of a man destined to shine in the midst of dangers, at the peaceful multitude of roofs cut in two by the brown tide of the stream. . . ." When Marlow visits him in Patusan they stand talking on the top of a hill. "He was like a figure set up on a pedestal, to represent in his persistent youth the power, and perhaps the virtues, of races that never grow old, that have emerged from the gloom." Even at his ignominious trial he stood elevated in the witness-box "and dark faces stare up at him from below." So much is obvious, perhaps too obvious. So perhaps are Conrad's pointers to the vulnerabilities and limitations inherent in Jim's characteristic heroic pose. His incurable taste for romantic day-dreams nourished on fictional situations, his incapacity for self-knowledge, even the physical fact of his being "an inch, perhaps two under six feet" with which the book all too significantly begins, make "the subtle unsoundness of the man" a somewhat less subtle thing than Conrad probably thought. Jim is all too obviously flawed. But his most crucial shortcoming is more interesting. It is hinted at in his first failure to take the opportunity for heroic action which offered itself while he was still a boy at the marine school. While he is indulging in heroic daydreams a real distress signal goes up and the young trainee-sailors have to effect a rescue. But active as he is in his dreams, when confronted by the real thing Jim is paralysed. "He stood still," Conrad uses the phrase twice, "as if confounded." This inability to act is more glaringly revealed on board the refugee ship *Patna*. The nature of the captain and other men who desperately work to lower one lifeboat for themselves with no thought for the hundreds of sleeping refugees is made very clear: they are base, cowardly animals (the skipper particularly is described in the most bestial terms) who, with no thought for dignity or duty, are galvanised into frantic efforts to save their skins. To Jim they are contemptible, loathsome fools involved in scenes of grotesque "low comedy." But Jim himself?—he simply doesn't move. "He wanted me to know he had kept his distance; that there was nothing in common between him and these men—who had the hammer. Nothing whatever. It is more probable he thought himself cut off from them by a space that could not be traversed. . . ." He does not do anything to alert the sleeping passengers, but he does not take part in the almost farcically crude attempts to lower that one shameful life-boat. He does nothing. He is the passive hero who is faced by scenes of macabre low-comedy and doesn't even know how or where to begin. He feels a shuddering contemptuous disdain for the men shamelessly acting on their basest motives—he wouldn't even touch a hammer. (But that hammer betokens action—and the procuring of the hammer was in fact an heroic act even if done for the basest motives.) And yet as Jim tells his story to Marlow it becomes a terrible case of *"qui s'excuse s'accuse."* He protests too much—that he has nothing in common with these men; yet when the pinch comes, when it seems as though he is really faced by the alternative of life and death, albeit an ignoble life and an heroic death, he suddenly finds that he has jumped, that he is down among those most contemptible of men. The space separating the butterfly and beetle—in men, in one man—can in fact be "traversed" —traversed in an instant. The physical descent is wonderfully apt for this is indeed a classic "fall." The heroic heights are abandoned: the butterfly is suddenly seen sprawling ingloriously among the beetles and an awful question arises. Has Jim at this moment found his true "level"?

We must leave Jim for a moment and consider the other objects of Stein's study—the beetles. Let us regard beetles as ugly earth-bound creatures, devoid of dignity and aspiration, intent merely on self-preservation at all costs: but gifted with a hard shell which serves them well in their unscrupulous will to live—to live on any terms, and capable of great malevolence when that life is threatened. There are hordes of such insects in *Lord Jim*. In fact one could describe the logic of Jim's continual flight as an attempt to escape from the beetles of mankind: and the drama of his travels is generated by the beetles who are continually crossing his path. Apart from the skipper of the *Patna,* who is in some ways the grossest beetle of them all, the most important are Chester, Cornelius, and Brown.

Chester is waiting for Jim after his trial like a morality play tempter. Jim's dishonour is symbolized by the cancelling of his certificate, and the punishment literally staggers him: he walks weakly away from the court. Immediately Chester appears to talk to Marlow—robust, healthy, tough, and contemptuous of all man-made standards.

> He looked knowingly after Jim. "Takes it to heart?" he asked scornfully. "Very much," I said. "Then he's no good," he opined. "What's all the to-do about? A bit of ass's skin. That never yet made a man. You must see things exactly as they are—if you don't, you may just as well give in at once. You will never do anything in this world. Look at me. I made it a practice never to take anything to heart." "Yes," I said, "you see things as they are."

From his conversation it is clear that Chester is a figure of vigour, resourcefulness, and endless energy of action: he is never enfeebled or immobilized by a sickly conscience. "The Lord knows the right and wrong of that story" is his typical comment on the rumor that his accomplice Robinson once indulged in cannibalism. As far as he is concerned, if Robinson ate human flesh to keep himself alive, then that does credit to his realistic turn of mind—he, too, saw things as they were. Chester offers Jim a job of dubious morality and Marlow refuses on Jim's account. Chester shrugs and leaves Marlow with this comment on Jim. "He is no earthly good for anything." Or as we might re-phrase it—he is no good for any earth-bound activity. And so it appears. Jim takes job after job and performs with great efficiency until a beetle turns up, usually with the story of the *Patna* and his own acrid comments on it. At various times Jim is explicitly or unconsciously called a cur, a skunk, a rat—all those repulsive animals with which the butterfly part of his nature least wishes to have anything to do. Cornelius turns up in more unusual circumstances. He is the lazy, sluggish, dilapidated father of the girl Jim loves in Patusan. He wretchedly mistreated his wife so that she died crying, and now he continues his indolent tyranny over the girl. He is a man who has gone morally to seed. But when Jim and the girl fall in love he asserts his odious presence. His base nature is wonderfully intimated in kinaesthetic terms by Conrad. Just to watch the man walk is to know him for what he is:

> Cornelius was creeping across in full view with an inexpressible effect of stealthiness, of dark and secret slinking. He reminded one of everything that is unsavoury. His slow laborious walk resembled the creeping of a repulsive beetle, the legs alone moving with horrid industry while the body glided evenly. I suppose he made straight for the place where he wanted to get to, but his progress with one shoulder carried forward seemed oblique. He was often seen circling slowly amongst the sheds, as if following a scent; passing before the veranda with upward stealthy glances; disappearing without haste round the corner of some hut.

He soils the air in which Jim is trying to work out his salvation, and seems to embody a repulsive but ineradicable presence. "He has his place neither in the background nor in the foreground of the story; he is simply seen skulking on its outskirts, enigmatical and unclean, tainting the fragrance of its youth and of its naiveness." But this man has a certain momentum of hate. And from his base perspective he sees the weakness of Jim. He tells his opinion to Marlow. "He is a big fool, honourable sir. . . . He's no more than a little child here—like a little child—a little child." With this insight (and the animus generated by Jim's refusal to give him money for his daughter) he knows enough to set about betraying and destroying Jim. In his own miserable way he *acts*. And Cornelius too has the lineaments of a figure in a morality play. "Somehow the shadowy Cornelius far off there seemed to be the hateful embodiment of all the annoyances and difficulties he [Jim] had found in his path." It is no use Jim's crying out "nothing can touch me" (they are almost his dying words), for somehow such foul presences as Cornelius always loom up to finger with soiled hands the weak spots in his honour. The most notable beetle however is Brown, the man who turns up unexpectedly and is directly responsible for Jim's downfall. As Marlow talks to him on his death bed it becomes clear that Brown feels a profoundly instinctual antipathy towards Jim, a hatred of him which is not accounted for by the narrative facts.

> "I could see directly I set my eyes on him what sort of a fool he was," gasped the dying Brown. "He a man! Hell! He was a hollow sham. As if he couldn't have said, 'Hands off my plunder!' blast him! That would have been like a man. Rot his superior soul! He had me there—but he hadn't devil enough in him to make an end of me."

The revulsion is mixed: Jim's air of moral superiority maddens Brown, as evidence of a superior ethic will always infuriate a man who lives by a baser one, for what Jim sees as a moral mission, his sacred obligation to the natives, Brown can only see as potential "plunder." On the other hand Jim's refusal to fight like a man, his incapacity for diabolical *action*, revolts the man of devilish energy. For Brown, Jim is repulsive because he pretends to be more than a man, and yet in his hollow inactivity he reveals himself to be devoid of all those attributes which make a man man-like. He is, thus, a "fraud." Brown's description of his crucial encounter with Jim brings the issues of the book to a head. Marlow paraphrases Brown's account:

> I know that Brown hated Jim at first sight. . . . he cursed in his heart the other's youth and assurance, his clear eyes and untroubled bearing. . . . And there was something in the very neatness of Jim's clothes, from

the white helmet to the canvas leggings and the pipeclayed shoes, which in Brown's sombre, irritated eyes seemed to belong to things he had in the very shaping of his life contemned and flouted.

Brown then recalls the exchange in his own words, an exchange, it should be remembered, which means life or death to Brown. " 'We are all equal before death,' I said. I admitted I was there like a rat in a trap, but we had been driven to it, and even a trapped rat can give a bite. He caught me up in a moment. 'Not if you don't go near the trap till the rat is dead.' " It is a typical answer—Jim still has an incurable distaste for any action which means involving himself with base, dirty people. He doesn't want to take a part in any low comedy, although we may recall that on one occasion Jim himself was described as a rat. But even as a rat he has no bite to him. Brown pursues his case with an amoral anarchic gusto which has a curious sort of unscrupulous heroism all its own ("a virile sincerity in accepting the morality and consequences of his acts"), and as he makes his points we seem to see Jim withering before our eyes.

> "And I would let you shoot me and welcome," I said. "This is as good a jumping-off place for me as another. I am sick of my infernal luck. But it would be too easy. There are my men in the same boat—and, by God, I am not the sort to jump out of trouble and leave them in a d—d lurch," I said. . . . "I've lived—and so did you though you talk as if you were one of those people that should have wings so as to go about without touching the dirty earth. Well—it is dirty. I haven't got any wings. I am here because I was afraid once in my life. Want to know what of? Of a prison."

Brown is strong because he can admit to fear without letting it undermine his mainsprings of action: he is strong because his element is the dirt of the world: he is strong because he lives by action (he only fears the arresting walls of a prison), and being a man of action he would never do the one thing which has soured Jim's life, leave his mates, abandon his ship. And Jim finally takes what is to Brown the easy way out and lets himself be shot. On his own terms Brown is "right"—he "sees things as they are" and therefore always acts with a prompt and savage confidence: (he feels the "lust of battle," an emotion foreign to Jim). And because of this he can get through Jim's faulty heroic armature and "shake his twopenny soul around and inside out and upside down." Perhaps Conrad makes the opposition between the two men too clear, but Brown is a convincing figure, the man of dirt who wishes to soil the disdainful immaculateness of Jim, the man of action who wishes to grab hold of that "don't-you-touch-me sort of fellow," the man without wings who yearns to drag down into his element those superior souls who think they can live without touching the earth. He has an Iago streak in him—the basic diabolical compulsion to bring everything to chaos, to reduce fine things to a mess: he has both the irresistible impulse and the requisite satanic insight to puncture the Othellos and Jims of this world. He is the anti-heroic, anti-idealistic supreme: and he is supremely successful because he has an uncanny instinct for attacking just those faults of self-deception and inaction and shame which mar Jim's armour of idealism. The moral to be drawn from Brown's unforeseeable and disastrous appearance in Jim's moral hide-out is not that a bad penny always turns up but that you can never get away from the beetles of this world, their amoral ferocity, and their murderous truth.

Before returning to Jim I want to draw attention to one of Conrad's most notable creations of the beetles of this world. I refer to Donkin in *The Nigger of the "Narcissus."* Once Conrad starts on his description of Donkin he can scarcely control himself. The torrential abuse certainly mars the texture of the book but it clearly reveals the author's preoccupation with this kind of man. I quote only certain key extracts.

> He looked as if he had known all the degradations and all the furies. He looked as if he had been cuffed, kicked, rolled in the mud; he looked as if he had been scratched, spat upon, pelted with unmentionable filth . . . and he smiled with a sense of security at the faces around. . . . His neck was long and thin; his eyelids were red; rare hairs hung about his jaws; his shoulders were peaked and dropped like the broken wings of a bird; all his left side was caked with mud which showed that he had lately slept in a wet ditch.

A broken-winged creature at home in the mud–Donkin is related to Brown.

> They all knew him. Is there a spot on earth where such a man is unknown. . . . He was the man who cannot steer, that cannot splice, that dodges the work on dark nights; that, aloft, holds on frantically with both arms and legs, and swears at the wind, the sleet, the darkness; the man who curses the sea while others work. . . . The independent offspring of the ignoble freedom of the slums full of disdain and hate for the austere servitude of the sea.

Donkin subsumes in his one person all the basest instincts and inclinations of man. He too has a devil of destruction in him, a rancorous feral hate for all the illusions which sustain and dignify mankind.

> He had a desire to assert his importance, to break, to crush; to be even with everybody for everything; to tear the veil, unmask, expose, leave no refuge—a perfidious desire of truthfulness!

That last word comes as something of a surprise, but Conrad means it. This emerges more clearly when Donkin starts trying to sow dissent among the sailors when the voyage gets rough: he complains about everything—discipline, work, pay; he denies the point of all effort. "His picturesque and filthy loquacity flowed like a troubled stream from a poisoned source." But the men listen: his "filthy loquacity" appeals to and elicits a response from all of them. "We abominated the creature and could not deny the truth of his contentions. It was all so obvious." Donkin is in complete command of one kind of truth, the beetle's truth, the truth that asserts that a certificate of duty is a mere piece of ass's skin, that ideals of conduct are "no earthly use," that honour is a fraud. For Conrad this was the abominable truth of the ditch. But it was a truth.

If this is the only kind of truth then Jim is a deluded fool indeed; but for Conrad Jim is something more complex and interesting. In a letter to Edward Garnett written in 1908 Conrad complains of his critics: ". . . there is even one abandoned creature who says I am a neo-platonist. What on earth is that?" Conrad disliked all facile classification, but against that outburst of astonishment we can put an extract from a letter to Sir Sidney Colvin written in 1917.

> I have been called a writer of the sea, of the tropics, a descriptive writer, a romantic writer—and also a realist. But as a matter of fact all my concern has been with the "ideal" value of things, events and people. That and nothing else. The humorous, the pathetic, the passionate, the sentimental *aspects* came in of themselves—*mais en vérité c'est les valeurs idéales des faits et gestes humains qui se sont imposés à mon activité artistique*. Whatever dramatic and narrative gifts I may have are always, instinctively, used with that object—to get at, to bring forth *les valeurs idéales*. Of course this is a very general statement but roughly I believe it to be true.

It is also a letter and must not be taken as a pondered creed—but the reiteration of the notion of "ideal value" is surely significant. Of course Conrad was not a systematic Platonist of any kind, but undoubtedly he had felt an urge to locate and identify a value which lay under the surface of certain people, actions or things, a value inaccessible to the beetles with their relentlessly accurate eye for the surface facts, their diabolical gift for seeing things "as they are." Jim is made a crucial focus of this inquiry, this question of the other truth. Is he just a child, a fool, a coward, a fraud? Or does he embody some sort of ideal value, no matter how debased that ideal may be by an involvement with the mud of the world? This takes us back to Marlow's interview with Stein. Stein habitually talks in ellipses and paradoxes and his speech is full of cryptic lacunae. Thus he mutters: "To follow the dream, and again to follow the dream—and so—*ewig—usque ad finem*. . . ." and more specifically on Jim: " 'He is romantic

—romantic,' he repeated. 'And that is very bad—very bad, . . . Very good, too,' he added." Then he throws at Marlow the question of why Jim exists so strongly for him. Marlow searches his mind. "At that moment it was difficult to believe in Jim's existence . . . but his imperishable reality came to me with a convincing, with an irresistible force! I saw it vividly, as though . . . we had approached nearer to absolute Truth, which like Beauty itself, floats elusive, obscure, half submerged, in the silent waters of mystery."

We have been taught to shy at capitalised abstractions in the novel and perhaps rightly—the passage is easily faulted. But it does reveal Conrad's intention, or perhaps we should say Conrad's problem. Jim stands for our best illusions, those exercises of the imagination which we allow to guide our conduct in order to give it purpose, dignity, and, in Conrad's word, glamour. It is our illusions, our ideals, which give us "gorgeous markings" and aspiring wings. Is there anything that can be called truth in them, do these "pure exercises of imagination" contain any of "the deep hidden truthfulness of works of art?" Such seems to be Marlow's line of questioning. Of course to have employed the persona of Marlow is a gesture of detachment, of possibly ironic disengagement on Conrad's part—the narrator examines his character, the author scrutinizes both; but in this early work it is hard to feel that Marlow's tentative Platonic musings are not in fact Conrad's own. When Marlow offers such remarks as: "the truth disclosed in a moment of illusion" or "our illusions, which I suspect only to be visions of remote unattainable truth, seen dimly," we inevitably feel that the author is backing him up to the hilt. Jim reminds Marlow—and, we feel, Conrad—"of those illusions you had thought gone out, extinct, cold": not everybody lives by illusions of course—"it is respectable to have no illusions—and safe—and profitable," but it is also "dull." Illusions redeem life momentarily from its dullness or dirtiness: they are responsible for "that light of glamour created in the shock of trifles, as amazing as the glow of sparks struck from a cold stone—and as short-lived, alas!" Are the illusions true? Marlow is vague—memorably vague: "he [Jim] felt . . . the demand of some such truth or some such illusion—I don't care how you call it, there is so little difference, and the difference means so little." From an author that would be unacceptable—from a genial after-dinner racounteur we let it pass. And we let it pass because a better sentence follows. "The thing is that in virtue of his feelings he mattered." The horizons Jim dreamed of are unattainable, the heroic deeds he imagined to himself he cannot realize in action, life consecrated to an ideal of conduct cannot be lived, not only because of the ungovernable hostility of baser men but also because of the inexpugnable weaknesses in the ideal itself.

But the feelings that lie at the root of all these aspirations and ideals—you cannot give the lie to those. Such would seem to be Marlow's point.

And it is because of the unflagging persistence of those feelings, their determination to operate at the highest attainable level, that both Marlow and Stein are inclined to speak of the "truth" of Jim's later life. When Jim's widow complains to Stein that Jim at the end was false, Stein answers with unusual emotion. "No! no! True! true! true!" and Marlow speaks, rather curiously, of "the sheer truthfulness of his last three years of life" as though, like the Great Gatsby, Jim had lived up to "his Platonic conception of himself." As Marlow says early in the book, he was aware of "an obscure truth" in Jim's attitude to life which seemed "momentous enough to affect mankind's conception of itself." Jim's conception of himself is vulnerable and romantic in the extreme and is responsible for culpable failures to act in the right way at the right time. But Conrad is obviously allowing him a poetic gloss, as though there is something he cannot, dare not, bring himself to utterly condemn. For this reason Marlow's account of Jim tries, at the end, to convince us that "his spirit seemed to rise above the ruins of his existence." But it is a weak gesture, and the last line of the novel has a melancholy ring to it. "Stein has aged greatly of late. He feels it himself, and says often that he is 'preparing to leave all this; preparing to leave. . . .' while he waves his hand sadly at his butterflies."

One can see *Lord Jim* as Conrad's regretful farewell to the butterflies. Like the actual butterfly which Stein shows Marlow in their first interview, Jim was the last of a dying species as far as Conrad was concerned. "Only one specimen like this they have in *your* London, and then—no more." For the terrible unavoidable truth about Jim is that "he is not good enough"—the worse truth to Conrad is that "nobody, nobody is good enough." Jim cannot triumph over the ugly *facts* (a key word in the novel) though he spends his time trying to: he cannot "lay the ghost" of the ugly fact that he himself embodies and must carry with him wherever he goes. And these ugly facts are beetle facts and together with the brute facts of an indifferent Nature they seem to have the malevolent desire "to annihilate all that is priceless and necessary." But these facts are true—which is why truth is always referred to as "painful" or "sinister" in the later Conrad. Jim, despite the Platonic halo and the author's efforts to shore him up poetically, is not finally true. Or not true enough for the relentlessly penetrating eye of Conrad. The realists have no ideals—thus their lives are ugly. But the idealist has no grip on reality: he cannot live properly at all. *Lord Jim* is a prelude to profound pessimism. Like

Winnie Verloc in *The Secret Agent* Conrad came to feel "profoundly that things do not stand much looking into." Unlike Winnie he cannot help continuing to look. And what he comes to see is an abysmal absence of meaning and value in the world. If E. M. Forster is right in saying that "the secret casket of his genius contains a vapour rather than a jewel," that is because Conrad felt that at the center of existence there was only a vapour, and not the much desiderated jewel. There is an arresting passage in a letter to Cunninghame Graham which refers to the last sentence of that writer's preface to *Mogreb-al-Acksa*. The sentence enigmatically implies that there is a safe and meaningful destiny at the end of the road somewhere just to the right of a lone tree on the horizon. Conrad comments:

> Ah! the lone tree on the horizon and then bear a little (a very little) to the right. Haven't we all ridden with direction to find no house but many curs barking at the heels. Can't miss it? Well, perhaps we can't. And we don't ride with a stouter heart for that. Indeed, my friend, there is a joy in being lost, but a sorrow in being weary. . . . But what business have you, O Man! coming with your uncomprehended truth,— a thing less than mist but black, to make me sniff at—the stink of the lamp? Ride to the tree and to the right,—for verily there is a devil at the end of every road. Let us pray to the poor belied gods, to gods with more legs than a centipede and more arms than a dozen windmills: let us pray to them to guard us from the mischance of arriving somewhere.

Arriving, that is, at the final truth which is "less than mist but black." It seems to me that Conrad reached that last stage of pessimism which very few other writers—Melville is one—have experienced. The stage at which the greatest fear is not that the meaning of life might be evil but that there might be absolutely no meaning at all to be found. It is easy to state it thus glibly: but to have that conviction gnawing at you for the better part of a life time must be a rare and unenviable experience. Which is perhaps why Conrad's letters are among the most anguished any writer has left to us. Such a man may well pray for the grace of non-arrival.

There is no time here for a full study of Conrad's pessimism but the conclusions which it seems to me that Conrad reached, however unwittingly and unwillingly, in *Lord Jim* throw an interesting light on two recurring themes of his work, namely, the experience of total darkness, and the more than nautical significance of "steering." It is commonly agreed that in many of his early works Conrad exhibits a rather facile predilection for melodramatic atmospherics: there is too much ineffable, ineluctable darkness, too much of the "tenebrous immensity" style of writing. But at certain key moments in his books the experience of utter darkness carries a profound moral and psychological significance. Jim really discovers the difficulty of living according to a preconceived ideal not when he makes the fatal jump —he does that in a mood of almost paralysed passivity—but when he is alone with the other base cowards in the complete darkness of the sea. The way he describes the experience is revealing. "After the ship's lights had gone, anything might have happened in that boat—anything in the world—and the world no wiser. . . . We were like men walled up in a roomy grave. No concern with anything on earth. Nobody to pass an opinion. Nothing mattered." And later: "But the lights. The lights did go! We did not see them. They were not there. If they had been, I would have swum back —I would have gone back and shouted alongside—I would have begged them to take me on board. . . ." He is referring to the lights of the abandoned ship, which would have told him that the ship was not sinking after all. But they mean more than that. They are clues to ethical conduct which the external world gives us, the signs which we have to interpret and then act upon, irresistible reminders from the world of men. Conrad is interested in those crucial moments when we are utterly "alone with ourselves," when to all intents and purposes nothing matters, when all the guidance must come from within, when all the lights have gone out. Jim claims that in such circumstances "there was not the thickness of a sheet of paper between the right and wrong of this affair" and "not the breadth of a hair between this and that." Marlow answers, rather mordantly, "It is difficult to see a hair at midnight." Impossible, we might concede. And it is exactly *then* that Conrad wants to know how a man behaves, how a man should behave, how he can find sanctions and supports to resist the insidious gravitational pull towards the base, beetle-like, irresistible argument that "nothing matters." The narrator of *The Shadow Line* goes through a similar experience. During the storm: "I was alone, every man was alone where he stood. And every form was gone, top, spar, sail, fittings, rails; everything was blotted out in the dreadful smoothness of that absolute night" and then: "both binnacle lamps were out. . . . The last gleam of light in the universe had gone." In such circumstances "the eye lost itself in inconceivable depths," or as we might more crudely put it, the moral eye has nothing to focus on. *That* is the testing time. Darkness is an all too easy short-cut to portentous effects but at certain moments Conrad manages to invest it with a compelling elemental terror and he does so, I think, because it symbolised for him a passionately felt philosophical darkness. At times it is as palpable and convincing as "The Cloud of Unknowing" and for similar reasons. Conrad also had an intimate acquaintance with

the experience of "the lacking of knowing." This subterranean doubt
and scepticism comes very near the surface of some of his letters:

> I have often suffered in connection with my work from a sense of un-
> reality, from intellectual doubt of the ground I stand on.
> Everyone must walk in the light of his own heart's gospel. No man's
> light is good to any of his fellows. That's my creed from beginning to
> end. That's my view of life—a view that rejects all formulas, dogmas
> and principles of other people's making. These are only a web of illu-
> sions.
> My task appears to me as sensible as lifting the world without that
> fulcrum which even that conceited ass, Archimedes, admitted to be neces-
> sary.

The fulcrum he lacks is the fulcrum of faith, the fulcrum of immovable
and clarified convictions: "There is no morality, no knowledge and no
hope: there is only the consciousness of ourselves which drives us about
a world that, whether seen in a convex or concave mirror, is always
but a vain and floating appearance." Given this view of the world then
any idealism seems as pointless "as though one were anxious about the
cut of one's clothes in a community of blind men." And yet Conrad
was deeply concerned about a man's moral dress even when he was
invisible to the rest of the world. The behavior of the crowd held no
interest for Conrad. And to the question, how should one behave in
the dark, he had one firm answer—you steer.

Thus extrapolated the idea is vague in the extreme, but let us return
to *The Nigger of the "Narcissus"* for a concrete image of this one
positive which Conrad fervently believed in. I refer to Captain
Singleton's behavior in the storm during which Donkin whines, complains, and incites the men to abandon a pointless and exacting duty.

> Apart, far aft, and alone by the helm, old Singleton had deliberately
> tucked his white beard under the top button of his glistening coat. Sway-
> ing upon the din and tumult of the seas, with the whole battered length
> of the ship launched forward in a rolling rush before his steady old eyes,
> he stood rigidly still, forgotten by all, and with an attentive face. In front
> of his erect figure only the two arms moved crosswise with a swift and
> sudden readiness, to check or urge again the rapid stir of circling spokes.
> He steered with care.

That last telling short sentence (short sentences are rare in Conrad
and always used for special emphasis) underlines the simple unques-
tioning dedication with which Old Singleton does what, in the circumstances, most needs to be done. It makes it seem as though he
were acting in unflinching compliance with a categorical imperative.
The particularly Conradian aspect of this conception of duty is the
fact that he can no longer produce the sanctions and proofs which

would justify and enforce the standards of conduct which he nevertheless feels to be "imperative." Singleton steers but without being able to see the final destination. Some people would say that such persistence was futile. Conrad had been in such a situation.

> Sufficient moral tenacity is all I pray for, not to save me from taking to drink, because I couldn't even if I wanted to, but from the temptation to throw away the oar. And I have known good men do that too, saying: "It's no use." Then was my turn to keep the boat head to sea for fourteen solid hours.

Singleton steers (Donkin, we recall, cannot steer): but this is not the kind of steering which Shaw meant when he made Don Juan in hell say: "To be in hell is to drift: to be in heaven is to steer." For Shaw, a social meliorist, meant that men and society should allow themselves to be guided by their best intelligence, the brain, "the organ by which Nature strives to understand itself." Shaw could see, or thought he could, the destination and wanted us to use our heads and hurry up getting there. But for Conrad the mind could be a curse, an inhibitor or interrupter of proper conduct. Cunninghame Graham once wrote to Conrad suggesting he create a Singleton figure with an education added. Conrad's reply is much to our point.

> But first of all—what education? If it is the knowledge of how to live, my man essentially possessed it. He was in perfect accord with life. If by education you mean scientific knowledge then the question arises— what knowledge? How much of it—in what direction? Is it to stop at plane trigonometry or at conic sections? Or is he to study Platonism or Pyrrhonism, or the philosophy of the gentle Emerson? Or do you mean the kind of knowledge which would enable him to scheme, and lie, and intrigue his way to the forefront of a crowd no better than himself? Would you seriously of malice prepense, cultivate in that unconscious man the power to think? Then he would become conscious,—and much smaller,—and very unhappy. Now he is simple and great like an elemental force. Nothing can touch him but the curse of decay,—the eternal decree that will extinguish the sun, the stars, one by one, and in another instant shall spread a frozen darkness over the whole universe. Nothing else can touch him—he does not think.

There is a good deal of the essential Conrad in that paragraph. As he wrote elsewhere: "It is impossible to know anything, tho' it is possible to believe a thing or two." Haunted by the impossibility of knowledge, Conrad could not accept the beetle—Donkin's view of things—and he renounced the fallible, if beautiful, butterfly-Jim conception of life: but he believed in Singleton and the value and necessity of keeping the hands to the wheel, the dignity of standing erect and uncomplaining in the storms of a hostile nature and the darkness of encircling doubt.

On *Lord Jim*

by Dorothy Van Ghent

Marlow's last view of Jim, on the coast of Patusan, is of a white figure "at the heart of a vast enigma." Jim himself is not enigmatic. The wonder and doubt that he stirs, both in Marlow and in us, are not wonder and doubt as to what *he* is: he is as recognizable as we are to ourselves; he is "one of us." Furthermore, he is not a very complex character, and he is examined by his creator with the most exhaustive conscientiousness; he is placed in every possible perspective that might help to define him. The enigma, then, is not what Jim is but what we are, and not only what we are, but "how to be" what we are.

Jim's shocking encounter with himself at the moment of his jump from the *Patna* is a model of those moments when the destiny each person carries within him, the destiny fully molded in the unconscious will, lifts its blind head from the dark, drinks blood, and speaks. There is no unclarity in the shape that Jim saw at that moment: he had jumped—it is as simple as that. But because the event is a paradigm of the encounters of the conscious personality with the stranger within, the stranger who is the very self of the self, the significance of Jim's story is *our own* significance, contained in the enigmatic relationship between the conscious will and the fatality of our acts. Jim's discovery of himself was a frightful one, and his solution of the problem of "how to be" was to exorcise the stranger in a fierce, long, concentrated effort to be his opposite. The oracle spoke early to Oedipus, too, in his youth in Corinth, telling him who he was—the man destined to transgress most horribly the saving code of kinship relations—and Oedipus's solution of the problem of "how to be" was the same as Jim's: he fled in the opposite direction from his destiny and ran straight into it.

Jim is one of the most living characters in fiction, although his presentation is by indirection, through Marlow's narrative; that indirection is itself uniquely humanizing, for we see him only as people can see each other, ambivalently and speculatively. He is nevertheless an extraordinarily simplified *type,* obsessed with a single idea, divested of all psychological attributes but the very few that concretize his relationship with his idea. The simplification is classical; it is a simplification like that of Aeschylus' Orestes, possessed by the divine command, and like that of Sophocles' Oedipus, possessed by his responsibility for finding out the truth. Conrad is able thus to imply a clear-cut formal distinction between the man and his destiny (his acts), even though he conceives destiny as immanent in the man's nature and in this sense identical with him. Here is Jim, "clean-limbed, clean-faced, firm on his feet, as promising a boy as the sun ever shone on," and there are his acts—the destruction of his best friend, the destruction of himself, the abandonment of the Patusan village to leaderlessness and depredation. Similarly Orestes and Oedipus, human agents simplified to a commanding ethical idea, are analytically separable from their destinies, the *anankē* or compelling principle fatally inherent in their acts. This subtle but tangible distinction between the human agent and his destiny allows the classical dramatists to orient clearly what we may call the metaphysical significance of the hero's career, the universal problem and the law of life which that career illustrates. We see the hero as an ideal human type (literally "idealized" through his devotion to an idea of ethical action); but his fate is pitiful and terrible —a fate that, if a man's deserts were to be suited to his conscious intentions, should fall only on malicious, unjust, and treasonable men; and the problem, the "enigma," thus raised is the religious problem of the awful incongruity between human intention and its consequences in action, between ethical effort and the guilt acquired through such effort; and the law—if a law appears—will be the law that justifies, to man's reason and feeling, that appearance of awful incongruity. Conrad's treatment of Jim's story is classical in this sense, in that he sees in it the same problem and orients the problem in the same manner.

"In the destructive element immerse," Stein says, voicing his own solution of the problem of "how to be." There is no way "to be," according to Stein, but through the ideal, the truth as it appears, what he calls "the dream," although it is itself "the destructive element." "Very funny this terrible thing is," Stein says,

"A man that is born falls into a dream like a man who falls into the sea. If he tries to climb out into the air as inexperienced people endeavour to do, he drowns—*nicht wahr?* . . . No! I tell you! The way is

to the destructive element submit yourself, and with the exertions of
your hands and feet in the water make the deep, deep sea keep you up.
So if you ask me—how to be? . . . I will tell you! . . . In the destructive element immerse."

Stein's words are but one outlook on the universal problem that is
Jim's, but it is the outlook dramatized in Jim's own actions. It is that
dramatized by Sophocles also. Oedipus "submitted" himself to his ideal
of the responsible king and citizen, self-sworn to the discovery of the
truth. It was the "destructive element," bringing about the terrible
revelation of his guilt. So also Jim submits himself to his dream of
heroic responsibility and truth to men, fleeing from port to port, and
finally to Patusan, to realize it. And, again, the ideal is the "destructive element," bringing about the compact with Brown (a compact
made in the profoundest spirit of the dream) and inevitably, along
with the compact, destruction. The irony is that Jim, in his destructiveness, was "true." This is the classical tragic irony: the incongruity and
yet the effective identity between the constructive will and the destructive act.

Whether Conrad goes beyond that particular tragic incongruity to
the other ancient tragic perception, of ennoblement through suffering,
is doubtful. The "enigma" that Marlow finds in Jim's career has this
other dark and doubtful aspect. When, at the end, after receiving
Doramin's bullet, "the white man sent right and left at all those faces
a proud and unflinching glance," is he really fulfilled in nobility in
our sight? Has his suffering, entailed in his long and strenuous exile
and his guilt and his final great loss, given him the knowledge, and
with the knowledge the nobility, which is the mysterious and sublime
gift of suffering? The answer is doubtful. We need to bring to bear
on it the fairly inescapable impression that the only character in the
book in whom we can read the stamp of the author's own practical
"approval" is the French lieutenant who remained on board the *Patna*
while it was being towed into port. The French lieutenant would not
have acted as Jim did in the last events on Patusan—indeed is inconceivable in the Patusan circumstances. If, in Conrad's implicit evaluation of his material, the French lieutenant represents the ethically
"approved" manner of action and the only one, Jim can scarcely
support the complete role of the tragic hero of the classical type, the
hero who achieves unique greatness through suffering. (The French
lieutenant suffers only for lack of wine.) For our notion of what
constitutes a "hero" is thus surely divided: if the French lieutenant's
heroism is the true heroism, Jim's is not, and conversely. No doubt the
division—and it seems to be real in our response to the book—is

associated with a division of allegiance on Conrad's part,[1] between
emotional allegiance to Jim's suffering and struggling humanity, in all
its hybristic aspiration, and intellectual allegiance to the code represented by the lieutenant, in all its severe limitation and calm obscurity.
With this division in mind, it is impossible to identify the "view of
life" in the book as a whole with Stein's view of life, impressive as
Stein is in his broad and enlightened sensitivity: for the French
lieutenant knows nothing of a "destructive element," and if he did—
which he could not—would doubtless think that to talk of "submit-
ting" oneself to it was sheer twaddle.

What intervenes between Conrad's ambivalent attitude toward Jim's
story and the attitudes of Aeschylus and Sophocles toward their sub-
jects is modern man's spiritual isolation from his fellows. Jim's isolation is profound, most profound and complete at that last moment
when he "sent right and left at all those faces a proud and unflinching
glance": here his aloneness in his dream—his illusion—of faith to
men is unqualified, for the material fact is that he has allowed a
brigand to slaughter Dain Waris and his party, and that he has left
the village open to ravage. Moral isolation provides a new inflection
of tragedy. Orestes freed Argos from a tyranny, and Oedipus freed
Thebes from a plague. Their guilt and suffering had a constructive
social meaning; they had acted for the positive welfare of the citizens;
and that social version of their heroism, internal to the dramas in
which they appear, is the immediate, literal basis of our (because it is
the citizen-chorus's) appraisal of their heroism. But Jim—to use parallel terms—destroys his city. Thus there is nothing structurally internal to Jim's story that matches the positive moral relationship, in the
ancient dramas, between the social destiny and the hero's destiny, the
relationship that is presented concretely in the fact that the hero's
agony is a saving social measure. There is nothing to mediate, prac-
tically and concretely, between Jim's "truth" and real social life, as a
benefit to and confirmation of the social context. Jim is alone.

And yet one asks, is his last act, when he "takes upon his head" the
blood-guilt, an atonement? If it were so, it would be atonement not in
quite the same sense that the madness and exile of Orestes and the
blinding and banishment of Oedipus were atonements, for these involved the restoration of community health, whereas Jim's final act
brings about (projectively) the destruction of the community—but in
the necessary modern sense, necessitated by the fact of the disintegration of moral bonds between men: an atonement for that social steril-

[1] Albert J. Guerard discusses this division of allegiance in his *Joseph Conrad* (New
York: New Directions, 1947).

ity, a sacrifice offered in the name of moral community. If it were so, Jim would still be, metaphorically speaking, the savior of the city. No doubt Sophocles, civic-minded gentleman, did not "approve" of Oedipus: when parricide and incest occur in the leading families, what are the rest of us to do? how is the world's business to be kept up decently? what model shall we look to? But the Greek cities were said to have carried on quarrels over the burial place of Oedipus, for his presence brought fertility to the land. So also the story of Lord Jim is a spiritually fertilizing experience, enlightening the soul as to its own meaning in a time of disorganization and drought; and Conrad's imagination of Jim's story has the seminal virtue of the ancient classic. . . .

In Conrad's austerely pessimistic work, the self stands already created, the possibilities are closed. Again and again, and finally on Patusan, a "clean slate" is what Jim thinks he has found, a chance to "climb out," to begin over, to perform the deed which will be congruent with his ideal of himself. "A clean slate, did he say?" Marlow comments; "as if the initial word of each our destiny were not graven in imperishable characters upon the face of a rock." The tension, the spiritual drama in Conrad, lie in a person's relation with his destiny. The captain in "The Secret Sharer" acknowledges his profound kinship with a man who has violently transgressed the captain's professional code (the man has murdered another seaman during a voyage, and murder at sea is, in Conrad, something worse than murder; whatever its excuses, it is an inexcusable breach of faith with a community bound together by common hazard); but by the acknowledgment he masters his own identity, integrates, as it were, his unconscious impulses within consciousness, and thereby realizes self-command and command of his ship. In contrast with the captain of "The Secret Sharer," Jim repudiates the other-self that has been revealed to him; at no time does he consciously acknowledge that it *was* himself who jumped from the *Patna*—it was only his body that had jumped; and his career thenceforth is an attempt to prove before men that the gross fact of the jump belied his identity.

James works through recognitions; the self-creating character in James develops by taking into consciousness more and more subtle relations—"seeing" more in a world of virtually infinite possibilities for recognition, and thus molding consciousness, molding himself. Conrad works through epiphanies, that is, through dramatic manifestations of elements hidden or implicit in the already constructed character. The difference of method is suggestive of the difference of world view: in James, the world ("reality" as a whole) being, as it were, an open and fluid system, essentially creative; in Conrad, a closed and

static system, incapable of origination though intensely dramatic in
its revelations. (Paradoxically, the environments in James's open world
are the closed environments of city and house, while those in Conrad's
closed world are those of the open, the mobile sea.) The word
"epiphany" implies manifestation of divinity, and this meaning of the
term can serve us also in analyzing Conrad's method and his vision,
if we think of the "dark powers" of the psyche as having the mysterious absoluteness that we associate with the daemonic, and if we
think mythologically of a man's destiny both as being carried within
him, and, *in effect*—since his acts externalize his destiny—as confront-
ing him from without.

The sunken wreck that strikes the *Patna* is one such epiphany in
Lord Jim, and this manifestation of "dark power" is coincident with
and symbolically identifiable with the impulse that makes Jim jump,
an impulse submerged like the wreck, riding in wait, striking from
under. Outer nature seems, here, to act in collusion with the hidden
portion of the soul. But Conrad's supreme mastery is his ability to
make the circumstance of "plot" the inevitable point of discharge of
the potentiality of "character." [2] The accident that happens to the
Patna is not merely a parallel and a metaphor of what happens to
Jim at that time, but it is the objective circumstance that discovers
Jim to himself. The apparent "collusion" between external nature and
the soul, that gives to Conrad's work its quality of the marvelous and
its religious temper, is thus, really, only the inevitable working out of
character through circumstance.

Another major epiphany is the appearance of Brown on Patusan.
The appearance of Brown is, in effect, an externalization of the complex of Jim's guilt and his excuses for his guilt, for he judges Brown
as he judged himself, as a *victim of circumstances* (the distinction is
radical) rather than as a character exposed by circumstances, at least
to be given that benefit of doubt which would discriminate intention
from deed, ethos from the objective ethical traits to be seen in a man's
actions. Therefore he gives Brown a "clean slate," a chance to "climb
out"—from himself! But Jim's compact with Brown is more than a
compact with his own unacknowledged guilt; it is at the same time,
and paradoxically, a lonely act of faith with the white men "out
there," the men of Jim's race and traditions, the men upon the sea
whose code he had once betrayed, the "home" from which a single
impulse of nerves had forever exiled him. Brown is the only white man
who has appeared on Patusan to put to test Jim's ethical community
with his race and his profession, and in "taking upon his head" re-

---

[2] Morton Dauwen Zabel points this out in his Introduction to *The Portable Conrad* (New York: The Viking Press, Inc., 1947).

sponsibility for Brown's honor, he is superbly "true" to that community. But his truth is, effectively, betrayal; it is "the destructive element." Since only a chance in thousands brings Brown to Patusan, again outer nature seems to have acted in collusion with the "dark power" within Jim's own psyche, in order to face him once more with his unacknowledged identity when he is in the full hybris of his truth and his courage. But again the apparent collusion is only the working out of character through circumstance.

The impossibility of escape from the dark companion within leaves a man more perfectly alone in this world because he has that companion—who is always and only himself. The physical settings of Jim's career concretize his isolation. In constant flight from the self that he reads on men's lips but that he refuses to acknowledge except as a freakish injustice of circumstances, and, as he flees, pursuing the heroic ideal which would reconstitute him in the ranks of men where his salvation lies (for, as Conrad says, "in our own hearts we trust for our salvation in the men that surround us"), he comes finally to Patusan, ascends the river to the heart of the island, unarmed (why carry a loaded revolver when it is only oneself that one must face?)—ascends, that is, the dark paths of his own being back to its source:[3] "thirty miles of forest shut it off."

The first description that Marlow gives of the interior of the island is of a conical hill that is "split in two, and with the two halves leaning slightly apart," and in his reminiscences he returns frequently to the image of the hill (it is, indeed, the hill up which Jim hauled the cannon, in his first great exploit when he won the faith of the natives and became their protector), particularly to a scene of moonlight when the moon is rising behind the fissured mass.

> On the third day after the full, the moon, as seen from the open space in front of Jim's house . . . rose exactly behind these hills, its diffused light at first throwing the two masses into intensely black relief, and then the nearly perfect disc, glowing ruddily, appeared, gliding upwards between the sides of the chasm, till it floated away above the summits, as if escaping from a yawning grave in gentle triumph. "Wonderful effect," said Jim by my side. "Worth seeing. Is it not?"
>
> And this question was put with a note of personal pride that made me smile, as though he had had a hand in regulating that unique spectacle. He had regulated so many things in Patusan! Things that would have appeared as much beyond his control as the motions of the moon and the stars.

On Marlow's last night on the island he sees the same spectacle again, but the mood is different, oppressive.

[3] The observation is made by Mr. Guerard in *Joseph Conrad,* cited above.

I saw part of the moon glittering through the bushes at the bottom of the chasm. For a moment it looked as though the smooth disc, falling from its place in the sky upon the earth, had rolled to the bottom of that precipice: its ascending movement was like a leisurely rebound; it disengaged itself from the tangle of twigs; the bare contorted limb of some tree, growing on the slope, made a black crack right across its face. It threw its level rays afar as if from a cavern, and in this mournful eclipse-like light the stumps of felled trees uprose very dark, the heavy shadows fell at my feet on all sides . . .

Together Jim and Marlow watch "the moon float away above the chasm between the hills like an ascending spirit out of a grave; its sheen descended, cold and pale, like the ghost of dead sunlight." Carried to the mind by the image of the fissured hill, with the suspiciously ghostlike moon floating out of the chasm, is the relentless solitude of Jim's fate. He is not only an outcast from his kind but he is also an outcast from himself, cloven spiritually, unable to recognize his own identity, separated from himself as the two halves of the hill are separated. And the rebounding moon, in which he has so much pride, "as though he had had a hand in regulating that unique spectacle," remains in the mind as a figure of the ego-ideal, even that ideal of truth by which, Marlow says, Jim approached "greatness as genuine as any man ever achieved": its illusionariness, and the solitude implied by illusion. At the end, after all—when the silver ring that is the token of moral community falls to the floor, and through Jim's "truth" his best friend has been killed and the village under his protection betrayed—Jim is only what he has been; he is of the measure of his acts. To be only what one has been is the sentence of solitary confinement that is passed on everyman. It is in this sense, finally, that Jim is "one of us."

Since Jim is "one of us," the truth about Jim will be—within the scope of the expressiveness of Jim's story—a truth about life; and in view of this responsibility, Conrad's task of evaluation demands that *all* the accessible evidence be presented and that it be submitted to mutually corrective hypotheses of its meaning. There are Jim's actions, which are concrete enough and simple as the concrete is simple. But the significance of action is significance in the judgments of men, which are various; and as soon as judgment is brought to the act, the act becomes not simple but protean. *What,* then, *is* the act? The question defines Conrad's method in this book, his use of reflector within reflector, point of view within point of view, cross-chronological juxtapositions of events and impressions. Conrad's technical "devices," in this case, represent much more than the word "device" suggests: they represent extreme ethical scrupulosity, even anxiety; for the truth about a man is at once too immense and too delicate to sustain any failure of carefulness in the examiner.

The omniscient early chapters give briefly the conditions of Jim's upbringing, his heroic dreams, two incidents in his sea training, the *Patna* voyage up to the moment when the submerged wreck strikes, and the courtroom scene with Jim in the dock: that is, the first chapters take us up to the point where the accused is placed before us and the processes of judgment have to begin. From here, Marlow takes over. Marlow is unofficial attorney both for the defense and the prosecution. He selects, objectifies, and humanizes the evidence on both sides, but he lets it—intensified and set in perspective through his intelligent, freely roaming curiosity—speak for itself. Marlow is the most familiar narrative mechanism in Conrad's work; and in this particular book *Marlow has to exist.* For Jim's "case" is not an absolute but a relative; it has a being only in relation to what men's minds can make of it. And Marlow provides the necessary medium of an intelligent consciousness, at once a symbol of that relativity, a concretization of the processes by which just judgment may be evoked, and—through his doubt and reverence—an acknowledgment of the irony of judgment of the relative.

The few particulars that are given of Jim's home environment are all we need to give the word "home" potency for this chronicle: there is the parsonage, its decency, its naïveté, its faith, its sterling morality, its representativeness of "the sheltering conception of light and order which is our refuge." In the thirty-fifth chapter, where Marlow takes final farewell of Jim, and Jim says,

> "I must stick to their belief in me to feel safe and to—to" . . . He cast about for a word, seemed to look for it on the sea . . . "to keep in touch with" . . . His voice sank suddenly to a murmur . . . "with those whom, perhaps, I shall never see any more. With—with—you, for instance."

the parsonage home, as well as the community of men upon the sea, contains the "those" with whom Jim must keep in touch through faithfulness in word and act. "Home" is the ethical code which enables men to live together through trust of each other, and which, in so binding them, gives them self-respect. The exclusiveness and naïveté of the parsonage background interpret the symbol of "home" in all its own relativity, its merely provisional status in the jungle of the universe. When we close the book, the symbol of "home" is as ghostlike as the moon over Patusan. But it is the only provision for salvation, in the sense in which Conrad uses the word salvation when he says, "In our own hearts we trust for our salvation in the men that surround us." The two incidents in Jim's early sea training, the storm in Chapter I, when he was "too late," and, in Chapter II, his disablement at the beginning of a hurricane week, when he "felt secretly glad he had not to go on deck," counterpoint his belief in himself with actualities of frustration. A certain distinct polarity is already established, between his dreams and the "facts"; and when, in Chapter II, Jim suddenly decides to ship as mate on the *Patna,* it is as if we saw a bar magnet curved into a horseshoe and bent until its poles closed, sealing personal will and the fatality of circumstances in a mysterious identity that is the man himself; for his unexplained choice of the *Patna* is in more than one sense a choice of exile. He could have gone back to the home service, after his convalescence; but he throws in his lot with the men he has seen in that Eastern port (and disdained) who "appeared to live in a crazy maze of plans, hopes, dangers, enterprises . . . in the dark places of the sea," and with those others who had been seduced by "the eternal peace of Eastern sky and sea," who talked "everlastingly of turns of luck . . . and in all they said—in their actions, in their looks, in their persons—could be detected the soft spot, the place of decay . . ." Moreover, on the *Patna* he is in a special sense a man alone, alone with a dream that is unsharable because he is among inferiors: the third chapter presents "the *Patna* gang" from Jim's point of view—"those men did not belong to the world of heroic adventure . . . he rubbed shoulders with them, but they could not touch him; he shared the air they breathed, but he was different . . ." Is his choice of the *Patna* a measure taken to protect his dream from reality? Is it thus significant of his "soft spot"? There is no choice but reality, and actually none but the single, circumscribed, only possible choice that is one's own reality—witnessed by Jim's jump from the *Patna,* as by his shipping on the *Patna* in the first place.

When Sophocles, in his old age, wrote of Oedipus again, he had Oedipus assert his innocence and curse those who had banished him; for Oedipus had acted in ignorance of the circumstances, and therefore could not be held guilty for them. Jim puts up a fight as Oedipus did, and the causes involved are the same: is the self deducible from circumstances? is one guilty for circumstances? is one guilty for oneself when one has no choice but to be oneself? is one guilty for oneself when one is in ignorance of what oneself is? if, with lifelong strife, one refuses to acquiesce in the self, is one guilty for the self? who has a right to pronounce this judgment?

Obviously from this point another device of presentation must be used, other than either objective presentation by the author or subjective presentation through Jim, for Jim is too youthful, idealistic, and ingenuous to throw light on himself, and "objectivity"—the objectivity of the camera and the sound recorder—is hopelessly inadequate to the

solution of these questions. Marlow has to take up the case, and Marlow—intelligent professional man of the sea, and insatiably curious
psychological observer—brings to bear on it not only Jim's own evidence (and his friendship with Jim draws from Jim much more than
he could ever say for himself—brings out gestures and tones, situations
and impulses, that only sympathy could bring out), and not only the
reactions of the judges (and the judges are more in number than those
in the courtroom), but also a marvelously sensitive registration of the
concrete detail of life, bits of color and form and movement, a chin, a
hand, a shuffle, a vase of dry flowers, a striped pajama suit, that could
not be admitted as "evidence" in a formal inquiry, but that are nevertheless essential psychological evidence to the sensitive investigator.

The *Patna* gang has to be presented over again, not now from Jim's
point of view but from Marlow's. So far as the *Patna* gang is concerned, the question is, is Jim one of them or "one of us"? Marlow has
only to see the group on a street corner to know that Jim is not one
of them; but he pushes further—he is around when the fat captain, in
his night-suit, squeezes into the ramshackle gharry and disappears,
"departed, disappeared, vanished, absconded; and absurdly enough it
looked as though he had taken that gharry with him." It is Marlow's
impression of the obscenely ridiculous captain that conveys to us the
captain's sur-reality: he is, through Marlow's view, not simply stupid
and inferior as he appeared to Jim, but a frightful manifestation of
underground evil, as mysterious and unaccountable in its apparition
as the captain's vanishing with the gharry is complete; that the captain wears a sleeping suit (like the murderer in "The Secret Sharer")
emphasizes the psychological, that is to say spiritual, symbolism of his
evil; he is another epiphany, a "showing" from the daemonic underground of the psyche—but he is only that, and the psyche, Jim's
psyche, is more than the obscene man in the sleeping suit.

Then Marlow interviews the chief engineer in the hospital, the
man with the noble head and the pink toads under his bed. The effort
is an effort again to test his perception that Jim is not one of them, but
"one of us"; for the initial perception alone is scarcely to be trusted,
since Jim, whatever his excuses, had identified himself with the *Patna*
gang by jumping from the ship. The pink toads under the chief
engineer's bed are a fearful inversion of Jim's own dream: they too
are a dream—and the dreamer has a noble head. The pink toads are
a horrible degeneration of the dream. They serve as a commentary on
the dream that cannot be evaded (no more than can the captain in
the sleeping suit). But Jim had stayed for the trial, while the captain
had disappeared, the chief engineer had cultivated the d.t.'s, and the
second engineer wasn't around (the little man will reappear later, for

the act is immortal). It is Jim's dream that makes him stay for the trial, and therefore Jim's dream cannot be identified with the chief engineer's, however identifiable they are in illusionary quality and spiritual potency. Marlow's visit with the chief engineer fixes this judgment of a difference, as well as of a similarity.

These two observations of Marlow's project the question of identity (the question "Who am I?" that is Oedipus' as well as Jim's), that can only be decided by comparison of like things and different things, discrimination of congruences and incongruences. Two identifications of Jim with other persons have been rejected—although even the impulse to distinguish suggests subtle similarities between the objects compared, and we can never forget that Jim was in the lifeboat with the *Patna* gang, though at the other end. The rest of the narrative moves through a devious course of identifications and distinctions. Brierly, the unimpeachable professional seaman, in some astounding way identifies himself with the accused man, Jim, and commits suicide. Is this another version of Jim's "jump"? If so, in avoiding by suicide the possibility of being Jim, Brierly succeeds merely in being what he was trying to avoid; this is Jim's "case" all over again. The loathsome Chester also identifies himself with Jim; Chester instantly spots him as the man for his job—fantastic exile on a guano island; "He is no earthly good for anything," Chester says,—"he would just have done for me"; the man has a "soft spot," and for men with a soft spot, as Jim himself had observed, "death was the only event of their fantastic existence that seemed to have a reasonable certitude of achievement"; for Chester, Jim is "one of us" in a sense that disgusts Marlow, and Marlow's disgust with Chester and therefore with Chester's appraisal of the man helps us to measure Jim: but the fact that Marlow, during those grueling hours in the hotel room when he is writing factitious letters in order to give Jim a chance for privacy with his ordeal, can hesitate between recommending Jim for a decent job and turning him over to Chester still suggests a doubt as to what "one of us" means, whether it has Chester's meaning or Marlow's.

The French lieutenant whom Marlow encounters, though he is a sympathetic man, does *not* identify himself with Jim; and curiously, while the French lieutenant represents the approved ethos of the profession (and not only of the profession of the sea, but of the profession of being human, as the author evaluates his material; for, in that evaluation, being human, as humans ought to be, *is* a profession, with an austere Spartan-like discipline),[4] he is the only person in the book who does not, in some way, identify himself with Jim except for Cornelius and Brown, who hate him as an opposite and as an indict-

[4] In his *Joseph Conrad*, Mr. Guerard thoroughly clarifies this issue.

ment of their evil (perhaps the captain of the *Patna* and the chief
engineer could be included here, but their presentation is more objective and their attitudes less determinable; although the same point
would hold): that is to say that the only cases in which subjective
identification with Jim does not take place are those of a man—the
French lieutenant—who is above Jim's failings by virtue of his mediocrity, and of men who are below Jim's problem by virtue of their
psychotic maliciousness. The portrait of the French lieutenant is extremely careful, as all the portraits in the book are done with extreme
care, for on the nature of the man who judges depends the validity of
the judgment.

> He clasped his hands on his stomach again. "I remained on board that
> —that—my memory is going (*s'en va*). Ah! *Patt-nà. C'est bien ça.
> Patt-nà. Merci.* It is droll how one forgets. I stayed on that ship thirty
> hours. . . ."

And just a moment before, we have learned that "all the time of
towing we had two quartermasters stationed with axes by the hawsers,
to cut us clear of our tow in case she. . . ." The French lieutenant's
failure to remember even the name of the ship, on which he had stayed
for thirty hours *after* Jim had jumped, and the laconic tone of the
information about the quartermasters' assignment, are a judgment of
Jim in terms of Jim's own dream. The French lieutenant's unconscious
heroism is the heroism that Jim had made a conscious ideal; and his
witness measures Jim's failure by the painful difference of fact. And
yet this damning commentary appears as inconclusive as that of the
pink toads under the chief engineer's bed; it is as far from and as near
to "the case."

The distinguished naturalist Stein offers another approach. Stein
has been a hero of action like the French lieutenant, but he is also a
hero of the intellect, and, in his way, a psychologist, a philosopher, and
an artist. Stein is able to identify himself with Jim through his own
profound idealism (as Marlow does through doubt). But Stein's idealism, so far as we know, has never differentiated itself from his actions;
he has the gift of nature which is itself ideal; he had known, Marlow
says, how "to follow his destiny with unfaltering footsteps." Stein
"diagnoses the case" of Jim, making it quite simple "and altogether
hopeless" by framing it in the question: "how to be." "I tell you, my
friend," he says,

> "it is not good for you to find you cannot make your dream come true,
> for the reason that you not strong enough are, or not clever enough.
> *Ja!*. . . And all the time you are such a fine fellow, too! *Wie?* . . . How
> can that be? . . ."

The shadow prowling amongst the graves of butterflies laughed bois-
terously.

Stein gives Jim his great chance to make his dream come true, by sending him to Patusan. This journey is ambiguous: "once before Patusan
had been used as a grave," Marlow reflects; while Stein prowls
"amongst the graves of butterflies," Brierly's remark about Jim recurs
to Marlow's mind: "Let him creep twenty feet underground and stay
there"; and there is the fissured hill at the heart of Patusan, whose
chasm is like a "yawning grave," from which the moon (the dream)
rises "like an ascending spirit out of a grave . . . like the ghost of
dead sunlight." The ancient mythical heroes, Odysseus and Aeneas,
made the "journey underground" to Hades in search of wisdom, and
brought it back to daylight—the wisdom which was knowledge of
their own destinies. And shadowily behind them is the barbarous
ritual that made a king by burying him and disinterring him, a sur-
rogate perhaps, or a "story" (mythos), to stand for the killing of an
old king and his "resurrection" in a new one. In the grave of Patusan
—"the secular gloom and the old mankind"—Jim's dream does come
true. But the doubt remains as to whether, like the ancient heroes, he
brought back to daylight the wisdom of his destiny—or, in other terms,
whether in that grave an old self was really buried and from it a
new one congruent with his dream was resurrected.

The test of daylight, of the bright sea beyond the dark island, offers
itself only through Brown. Jim identifies himself with Brown in two
ways, through his guilt, and through his honor: Brown is at once the
"dark power" in Jim's psyche and his only effective bond with the
brightness outside himself, the community of tradition to which "we
trust for our salvation." Brown's ambivalence for Jim is Jim's own
ambivalence, and it is, in its most extensive sense, the ambivalence
that exists in all historical and personal stages of experience where
law (the "code") and the self question each other—as well in the
Athens of Thucydides and Euripides as in our own time, and as well,
we must surmise, in Conrad as in Jim. The tale Conrad prepared to
narrate was a tale in the manner of the older classical dramatists,
wherein law—whether divine, as with Aeschylus, or natural, as with
Sophocles—is justified to the self, whatever its agonies of discovery.
But he managed to do a tale that put both the law and the self to
question, and left them there. At the end (dated July 1900), Stein does
not help:

> Stein has aged greatly of late. He feels it himself, and says often that he
> is "preparing to leave all this; preparing to leave . . ." while he waves
> his hand sadly at his butterflies.

Sympathy and Judgment in *Lord Jim*

by Albert J. Guerard

The . . . central preoccupation of Conrad's technique, the heart
of the impressionist aim, is to invite and control the reader's identifications and so subject him to an intense rather than passive experience.
Marlow's human task is also the reader's: to achieve a right human
relationship with this questionable younger brother. Marlow must
resist an excessive identification (which would mean abandoning his
traditional ethic); he must maintain a satisfactory balance of sympathy
and judgment. No easy task, since Jim demands total sympathy. "He
wanted an ally, a helper, an accomplice. I felt the risk I ran of being
circumvented, blinded, decoyed, bullied, perhaps, into taking part in
a dispute impossible of decision if one had to be fair to all the phantoms in possession—to the reputable that had its claims and to the
disreputable that had its exigencies." And this is, far more than in
most novels, the reader's moral drama and situation: to be subjected to
all the phantoms in possession, to be exposed to a continuous subtle
and flowing interplay of intellectual appeals to his judgment and
poignant appeals to his sympathy.

The reader must survive this experience and go through this laby-
rinth of evidence without the usual guide of an omniscient author or
trustworthy author-surrogate. The reader (looking incorrigibly for the
author's convictions and final decision) is likely to put his trust in
Marlow, including the Marlow who speaks of Jim's "greatness,"
"truth," and "constancy." But he does so at his peril. Or he may put
his trust, even more dangerously, in Stein, Jim's fellow-romantic.
Stein's wise and assured tones and his central position in the novel,
geographically speaking, have led many readers to assume that he conveys the author's judgment. It would be much more accurate to say

that Conrad's moral judgment is isolated, if anywhere, in the austere nameless "privileged man" of Chapter XXXVI, and that his uncorrected sympathy is isolated in Stein. (The "privileged man" would not admit that Jim had mastered his fate, and maintained "that we must fight in the ranks or our lives don't count.") Then to whom and to what should the reader attend, if not to his professed guides? The answer of course is that he should attend, eagerly yet skeptically, to everything: to the moralizing of the guides, yes, but even more to every scrap of evidence they offer by way of anecdote, digression, example. The reading of this novel is a combat: within the reader, between reader and narrators, between reader and that watching and controlling mind ultimately responsible for the distortions.

Doubtless the common impression left by a first reading is that the formal rational evidence is preponderantly favorable to Jim, and that the novel finally reaches a lenient verdict, even a judgment of "approval." Jim emerges as, simply, a hero and a redeemed man. But the evidence (as we discover on rereading) is by no means preponderantly favorable; and *Lord Jim* is as much a novel about a man who makes excuses as a novel that makes excuses. Our first impression that the novel "approves" Jim turns out to derive not from the area of rational evidence and judgment but from the area of novelistic sympathy; we discover, as we look a little more closely, that Marlow has repeatedly taken us in. He is a considerably more lenient witness than his austere moralizing tone suggests. On various occasions he brings in the damaging evidence (he is, after all, obliged to bring it in) very casually and digressively, as though inviting us to overlook it. So too, when we are inclined to judge harshly, Marlow diverts our attention from the suffering, "burning" Jim to those who merely rot in the background, or who live safely in a world of untested rectitude. "You've been tried." Jim has, at least, been tested and tried. Therefore he exists. Marlow evokes both sympathy and a more lenient judgment whenever he reminds us of those who are safe: Marlow's listeners, or Jim's father sending his four-page letter of "easy morality and family news," or the tourists in the Malabar Hotel where Jim begins his story. Their irrelevance colors our response to Jim's very questionable denial that he was afraid of death: "They were exchanging jocular reminiscences of the donkeys in Cairo. A pale anxious youth stepping softly on long legs was being chaffed by a strutting and rubicund globe-trotter about his purchases in the bazaar. 'No, really —do you think I've been done to that extent?' he inquired very earnest and deliberate." When we return to Jim a moment later, we listen to him more attentively: " 'Some of the crew were sleeping on the number one hatch within reach of my arm,' began Jim again."

Such sudden corrective juxtaposition is at once the novel's characteristic way of redressing a balance of meaning and its chief way of
moving us emotionally. It may operate in both directions, of course:
correcting an excessive austerity of judgment or correcting an excessive
sympathy. The matter is not easy to sum up, and my conclusion is
perhaps debatable. But here is it: that on a first reading we are inclined to think Marlow's own judgment of Jim too harsh (since we
have missed some of the evidence that led him to that judgment); that
on a second reading (because we are discovering that evidence with
a force of delayed impact) we may think Marlow's judgment too lenient. In other words, the unfavorable evidence that Marlow had half-
concealed through deceptive casualness of manner grows upon us at a
second or third reading, and becomes more difficult to discount. But
meanwhile our natural sympathy for Jim—the center of attention, the
man on the rack, the conscientious sinner, the man who has been
"tried"—has correspondingly diminished. . . .

The delicate interplay of sympathy and judgment, managed with
such ease in the novel itself, is difficult to describe. We may take, as an
example of crucial evidence within deceptively unemphasized digression, the testimony of the Malay helmsman in Chapter VIII. For some
pages we have listened to Jim's own vivid account of his emotions
after looking at the bulging bulkhead, and to Marlow's slightly more
distant and meditative retelling; together they have taken us as close
as we ever come to the original experience of quite understandable
fear. We are *there* as Jim, thinking the ship may go at any moment,
struggles with the pilgrim importuning him for water to drink; as
back on the bridge he finds the officers trying to get one of the boats
off the chocks. And at the moment of Jim's most urgent appeal for
both sympathy and understanding—"Where was the kindness in making crazy with fright all those people I could not save single-handed
—that nothing could save?"—Marlow characteristically withdraws to
comment on Jim's longing for ally, helper, accomplice.

In the next paragraphs Marlow holds a very fine balance: reminding us of Jim's self-deceptions and weakness but also of his conscientious shame, magnifying the struggle through allusion and analogy,
admitting his own allegiance. The effect at a first reading is to transfer our attention from Jim's dubious acts on board the *Patna* to the
magnitude of his present "dispute with an invisible personality."
When at last we get back to the *Patna*, Marlow not Jim does the telling, and we can see Jim, a not wholly ignoble figure, standing apart
from the other officers and the boat. "The two Malays had meantime
remained holding to the wheel"—only thoughtless, immobile figures,
not even part of our moral universe. We are quickly diverted from

them by the stunning retrospective information that the ship didn't sink. "And still she floated! These sleeping pilgrims were destined to accomplish their whole pilgrimage to the bitterness of some other end." Marlow remarks, casually, that the behavior of the two helmsmen was not "the least wonder of these twenty minutes."

We then move away from the *Patna* to the inquiry, where the two helmsmen were questioned, as for relief from dramatic and moral intensity. It is a moment for attention to flag. The first helmsman, when asked what he thought of matters at the time, says he thought nothing. The second "explained that he had a knowledge of some evil thing befalling the ship, but there had been no order; he could not remember an order; why should he leave the helm?" And the evidence he gives—if we attend to it, as we do on later readings—pricks Jim's balloon. Not the man on the rack and tortured sinner but the old Malayan helmsman devoted to and formed by the honest traditions of the sea is heroic. He defines himself when he pours out the names of skippers and ships. We are reminded of Conrad's pride in "these few bits of paper, headed by the names of a few Scots and English shipmasters."

> "To some further questions he jerked back his spare shoulders, and declared it never came into his mind then that the white men were about to leave the ship through fear of death. He did not believe it now. There might have been secret reasons. He wagged his old chin knowingly. Aha! secret reasons. He was a man of great experience, and he wanted *that* white Tuan to know—he turned toward Brierly, who didn't raise his head—that he had acquired a knowledge of many things by serving white men on the sea for a great number of years—and, suddenly, with shaky excitement he poured upon our spell-bound attention a lot of queer-sounding names, names of dead-and-gone skippers, names of forgotten country ships, names of familiar and distorted sound, as if the hand of dumb time had been at work on them for ages. They stopped him at last." (Chapter VIII)

Marlow refers to the helmsman rightly as an "extraordinary and damning witness." But he is silenced, in the novel, very quickly indeed. And we are taken back to the ship. There follow thirty-five pages of a detailed and tormented account of Jim's last minutes on board, of his jump "into an everlasting deep hole," of his harrowing time in the lifeboat with the "three dirty owls" and his day spent apart from them under a burning sun, deliberating whether to die. The reader cannot fail to take Jim's part against theirs, and is more and more tempted to take seriously his assertion that it was not *he* who had jumped. "I told you I jumped; but I tell you they were too much for any man. It was their doing as plainly as if they had reached up with a boathook and pulled me over." By the end of Chapter XI, recollecting his debates on suicide, Jim has again threatened to convert the *Patna* episode into an entirely interior affair.

Hence it is high time we return to material matters, to physical things and acts: to what might and might not have been done. And Marlow sweeps us ahead more than three years to his meeting with the French lieutenant of Chapters XII and XIII, who is perhaps the most damning witness and reflector of all. He too appears very casually, within a nominal digression, and I understand he is discounted by some readers as a stuffy and uninteresting figure. Marlow, who in these chapters clearly diverges from Conrad, would have liked so to dismiss him. But his role in the novel may be as crucial as Stein's; the scenes are in a way pendant. For Stein, the intellectual and dreamer who is also a successful man of action, Jim is "romantic"—which is very bad and "also very good." His dream and his anguish are what make him exist. But the French lieutenant, a moving figure of professional competence and integrity, and a man certainly capable of sympathy, at once calls attention to something else: Jim "ran away along with the others." Marlow the observer professes to be irritated by his stolid assurance. But Conrad obviously finds him both likable and admirable, and he has (like a Hemingway figure[1]) the esoteric wound betokening virtue:

"This was absolutely the first gesture I saw him make. It gave me the opportunity to 'note' a starred scar on the back of his hand—effect of a gunshot clearly; and, as if my sight had been made more acute by this discovery, I perceived also the seam of an old wound, beginning a little below the temple and going out of sight under the short grey hair at the side of the head—the graze of a spear or the cut of a sabre. He clasped his hands on his stomach again. 'I remained on board that—that—my memory is going (*s'en va*). Ah! Patt-nà. *C'est bien ça. Patt-nà. Merci.* It is droll how one forgets. I stayed on board that ship thirty hours.' " (Chapter XII)

Time "had left him hopelessly behind with a few poor gifts . . ." But, unlike Jim, he had done what had to be done. And of the thirty hours during which he remained on board the *Patna*, with two quartermasters stationed with axes to cut her clear of the tow if she sank, he chiefly remembers with irritation having had no wine to go with his food. He too was aware of the chief sources of danger, panic among the pilgrims and the "villainous" bulkhead. But he saw them as matters to be taken care of. The way to behave in crisis is to act efficiently. His words are distantly echoed, from one language to another, by Stein's account of an ambush:

[1] For instance, the arrow wound of the count in *The Sun Also Rises*.

". . . this manoeuvre eased the strain on the bulkhead, whose state, he expounded with stolid glibness, demanded the greatest care (*exigeait les plus grands ménagements*)." (Chapter XII)

"It was a little intrigue, you understand. They got my poor Mohammed to send for me and then laid that ambush. I see it all in a minute, and I think—This wants a little management. My pony snort, jump, and stand, and I fall slowly forward with my head on his mane." (Chapter XX)

At the end of the interview with the French lieutenant, Marlow is "discouraged about Jim's case." Earlier—noting the lieutenant's admission that everyone experiences fear, and his acknowledgment that Jim "might have had the best dispositions"—Marlow was glad to see him take "a lenient view." A suspicious reader might even suppose the lieutenant had begun to confess, on the preceding page, to an act of cowardice similar to Jim's. But the lieutenant means to do no such thing, and he does not take a lenient view. For he has "no opinion" as to what life is like when honor is gone. Hence he has not *acted* in cowardice. "I was confronted," Marlow says,

"by two narrow grey circlets, like two tiny steel rings around the profound blackness of the pupils. The sharp glance, coming from that massive body, gave a notion of extreme efficiency, like a razor-edge on a battle-axe. 'Pardon,' he said, punctiliously. His right hand went up, and he swayed forward. 'Allow me . . . I contended that one may get on knowing very well that one's courage does not come of itself (*ne vient pas tout seul*). There's nothing much in that to get upset about. One truth the more ought not to make life impossible . . . But the honour —the honour, monsieur . . .' " (Chapter XIII)

We do not, even after this second damning witness has spoken, get back to the Malabar House and Jim's narrative at once. Another reflector and witness appears, by way of a digressive development of a modifying clause: Bob Stanton. Marlow has been speaking of Jim's unglamorous mode of life as a water-clerk for De Jongh. Or is the business of an insurance canvasser, which "Little Bob Stanton" had been, even less glamorous? As with the French lieutenant, the introduction is casual and faintly ironic. And then we are told, as though it had no bearing on Jim's case, the story of Stanton's drowning while trying to save a lady's maid in the *Sephora* disaster. He too had done what had to be done. As chief mate he would leave no one on board a sinking ship; Jim had left eight hundred. Stanton reminds us of what the officer is expected to do, irrespective of temptation or mitigating circumstance. And at this point (after seventeen pages of damaging evidence in the guise of digression) we return to Jim and his heroic introspections. "Clear out! Couldn't think of it," he replies, when

Marlow offers Brierly's plan of escape. But we are less impressed than we would have been before listening to the French lieutenant and before hearing of Stanton's death.

The natural unreflective heroism of the French lieutenant and Stanton thus help to put Jim's reveries of heroism, and his actual failures and excuses, into a clearer perspective. We must remember that in every chapter and on every page the double appeal to sympathy and judgment is made, though one or the other may dominate; we are not being subjected to the blunt regular swings of a pendulum. Still, this is perhaps the point in the first part of the novel where our view of Jim is most severe. The following chapter sets in a strong returning flow of sympathy. We see Jim's formal punishment delivered in a "chill and mean atmosphere. The real significance of crime is in its being a breach of faith with the community of mankind, and from that point of view he was no mean traitor, but his execution was a hole-and-corner affair." In a sense a proper judgment has been passed on Jim's romantic ego and his vulnerable idealism: *certificate canceled.* Then, and almost at once, we see Jim's version of "how to be" in the very different perspective of Chester's gross cynicism: Chester who wants someone "no good" for his guano island, and who regards Jim as "no good" because he takes his downfall to heart. "You must see things exactly as they are"—as Chester's partner Robinson did, who ate his comrades rather than starve, and afterward showed no remorse.[2] Marlow does not accept Chester's proposal. But he vivifies it sufficiently to make us more sympathetic with Jim's plight. And again, though in Marlow's imagination only, we have the "secret sharer" image of the guilty man alone under a burning sun: "I had a rapid vision of Jim perched on a shadowless rock, up to his knees in guano, with the

[2] *Lord Jim* explores the fine distinctions between guilt and sense of disgrace yet remains ambivalent toward the character who—accepting what he has done as done—lives without remorse. Stein is such a man. But so too is Robinson, who three weeks after his rescue "was as well as ever. He didn't allow any fuss that was made on shore to upset him; he just shut his lips tight, and let people screech. It was bad enough to have lost his ship, and all he was worth besides, without paying attention to the hard names they called him."

In this connection, and though it may reflect only one of several moods, an 1891 letter from Conrad to Marguerite Poradowska is of interest: "Each act of life is final and inevitably produces its consequences in spite of all the weeping and gnashing of teeth and the sorrow of weak souls who suffer as fright grips them when confronted with the results of their own actions. As for myself, I shall never need to be consoled for any act of my life, and this because I am strong enough to judge my conscience rather than be its slave, as the orthodox would like to persuade us to be" (*Letters of Joseph Conrad to Marguerite Poradowska, 1890–1920,* translated and edited by John A. Gee and Paul J. Sturm [New Haven, 1940], p. 36).

screams of sea-birds in his ears, the incandescent ball of the sun above his head; the empty sky and the empty ocean all a-quiver, shimmering together in the heat as far as the eye could reach." The classic Promethean image of unending punishment magnifies Jim's suffering; it reminds us too of the moral isolation into which he will now enter more deeply than before. And the section ends (Chapters XV, XVI, XVII) with the not unsympathetic picture of Jim's long silent struggle with himself, while Marlow writes letter after letter. "He was rooted to the spot, but convulsive shudders ran down his back; his shoulders would heave suddenly. He was fighting, he was fighting—mostly for his breath, as it seemed." The "idea obtrudes itself that he made so much of his disgrace while it is the guilt alone that matters." Nevertheless the impression left, at the end of this part, is of a kind of stubborn courage.

This then is *Lord Jim's* chief way of provoking in its readers a strong human response and meaningful conflict: to interweave or suddenly juxtapose (rather than group logically and chronologically) the appeals to judgment and sympathy, to criticism and compassion. A man is what he does, which in Jim's case is very little that is not equivocal. But also he "exists" for us by the quality of his feeling and the poignant intensity of his dream. He is not "good enough" (as Marlow tells Jewel, as the Malay helmsman and other witnesses verify) yet his childish romanticism may be preferable to a cynical realism. In any event, as Marlow goes on to say "nobody is good enough." This is not a relativistic conclusion. It reminds us rather how strong Marlow's moral and community engagement was, against which his brotherly and outlaw sympathy contended.

These peculiar groupings—of incident and witness and evidence, of intellectual and emotional appeal—distinguish *Lord Jim* from most earlier fiction. But imagery also leaves us in provisional and perhaps lasting uncertainty. Is Jim "in the clear"? The novel's chief recurrent image is of substance and reality obscured, often attractively so, by mist or by deceptive light. *Fog, mist, cloud,* and *veil* form a cluster with *moonlight,* and with *dream,* to dramatize certain essential distinctions: between the conscious mind and the unconscious, illusion and reality, the "ego-ideal" and the self's destiny as revealed by its acts. Imagery is supposed to reveal an author's ultimate and perhaps unconscious bias. But much of the imagery here is grouped fairly consciously as part of a multiple appeal to the reader. These images—if they do form a cluster, if we do properly take them together—should help determine the delicate relationship of idealism and self-deception.

And hence they should help us to evaluate Stein's advice ("follow the dream") and Jim's ultimate conduct in Patusan, when opportunity comes to his side, veiled like an Eastern bride.

At a first reading all this imagery of nebulosity may magnify and glamorize Jim (as fog magnifies Wordsworth's sheep), and also may be partly responsible for our first impression that Jim is an exceedingly mysterious person. But its later effect may be to persuade us that Stein is not, unequivocally, a spokesman for the author, and to throw still further doubt on Jim's "redemption" in Patusan. "I ask myself whether his rush had really carried him out of that mist in which he loomed interesting if not very big, with floating outlines—a straggler yearning inconsolably for his humble place in the ranks."

The meaning of *mist*, as we look at its various appearances, is clearer than we might have expected. It can refer generally to ambiguity but more centrally refers to the aura of deception and self-deception that surrounds Jim's reality. Now and then Marlow has a "glimpse through a rent in the mist in which he moved and had his being," as Jim says something truly revealing: as he tells of his impulse to go back to the spot of the *Patna's* abandonment, or as he recognizes the good Marlow does him by listening. But the mists close again at once when Jim refers to his plight as "unfair." Thus we may call the mist his illusion of self or ego-ideal, which is in turn responsible for the deceptions; it may impose the "mask" of a "usual expression." Reality can then appear in an "unconscious grimace," or through rifts caused by the inward struggles. He stumblingly reveals the truth; or, we stumble upon it. "The muscles round his lips contracted into an unconscious grimace that tore through the mask of his usual expression—something violent, short-lived, and illuminating like a twist of lightning that admits the eye for an instant into the secret convolutions of a cloud." The provocative reality in this instance was a fact normally evaded: that he was in the lifeboat with the others. Or, "The mist of his feelings shifted between us, as if disturbed by his struggles, and in the rifts of the immaterial veil he would appear to my staring eyes distinct of form and pregnant with vague appeal like a symbolic figure in a picture." This questionable sentence would suggest that the "real" Jim behind the apparent one has the vague symbolic appeal. Very possibly this dubious phrasing simply came to Conrad, who refused to examine it closely.

Still, we can say that mist, fog, and veil conceal or blur reality. So too does moonlight, whose "occult power" can rob things of their reality: "It is to our sunshine, which—say what you like—is all we have to live by, what the echo is to the sound: misleading and confusing whether the note be mocking or sad. It robs all forms of matter—which, after all, is our domain—of their substance, and gives a sinister reality to shadows alone." Dorothy Van Ghent advances an interesting argument: that the split conical hill on Patusan suggests Jim's spiritual cleavage, and the moon rising between the two halves suggests a "figure of the ego-ideal" with its "illusionariness, and the solitude implied by illusion." [3] The moonlight of Patusan is certainly associated with immobility and isolation, and with times when Jim is seriously entranced by his pride and illusions of success. This moonlight comments on the unreality of his aspirations. So too (when Jim still confuses guilt and disgrace, and thus comes "no nearer to the root of the matter") Marlow notes the "irresistible slow work of the night settling silently on all the visible forms, effacing the outlines . . ." But if the light of the moon is associated with illusion and a blurring of reality, the dark of the moon can be a very important reality, and one largely responsible for our acts: the unconscious itself. "He appealed to all sides at once—to the side turned perpetually to the light of day, and to that side of us which, like the other hemisphere of the moon, exists stealthily in perpetual darkness, with only a fearful ashy light falling at times on the edge." Whatever their sympathies in the matter, Marlow and Conrad clearly believe that we shall be saved by the sunlight of action and that deceptive half-lights are menacing.

All this (if we are to trust Marlow at all) has an important bearing on Stein's ambiguous advice: to submit yourself to the "destructive element" of the ego-ideal; to attempt through action to realize (or live with?) that illusion of self; to "follow the dream." Jewel remarks, very accurately, that Jim "had been driven away from her by a dream." Marlow's introduction ("one of the most trustworthy men I had ever known") together with Stein's grave tones and the memorably cryptic quality of his utterance create an initial confidence. At a first reading we naturally identify Stein's judgment and Conrad's. But the imagery which occurs to Marlow, immediately after Stein gives his advice, seems to say something very different. It associates Stein and his "conviction" with the half-lights of deception and menacing illusion; it brings Stein down to Jim's level rather than raises Jim to his. We cannot be sure what Conrad thought about Stein. Neither, possibly, could Conrad himself. This is Marlow's comment:

"The whisper of his conviction seemed to open before me a vast and uncertain expanse, as of a crepuscular horizon on a plain at dawn—or was it, perchance, at the coming of the night? One had not the courage

[3] Dorothy Van Ghent, *The English Novel*, p. 237. This may be true, though the split hill exists in the "source" of Brooke's memoirs. The imagination makes its significant selections from reality. [Dorothy Van Ghent's essay is reprinted in this volume—ed.]

to decide; but it was a charming and deceptive light, throwing the impalpable poesy of its dimness over pitfalls—over graves. His life had begun in sacrifice, in enthusiasm for generous ideas; he had travelled very far, on various ways, on strange paths, and whatever he followed it had been without faltering, and therefore without shame and without regret. In so far he was right. That was the way, no doubt. Yet for all that the great plain on which men wander amongst graves and pitfalls remained very desolate under the impalpable poesy of its crepuscular light, overshadowed in the center, circled with a bright edge as if surrounded by an abyss full of flames. When at last I broke the silence it was to express the opinion that no one could be more romantic than himself." (Chapter XX)

"One had not the courage to decide . . ." The passage, which sounds perilously close to deliberate double talk, probably owes some of its ambiguity to Conrad's inner conflicts. For here the idealist, the skeptic, and the outlaw ("strange paths . . . without regret") all have their say. The ambiguity of Stein's remarks on the "destructive element" (which have regrettably come to mean anything any casual reader wants them to mean) may derive from the same conflicts. Conrad wants both the dreamer and the man who acts to survive: ". . . with the exertions of your hands and feet in the water make the deep, deep sea keep you up." But there is also a rhetorical ambiguity in the famous passage, which derives from our habit of thinking of the ideal or the illusory as "higher," and of air as higher than water. This is no doubt one reason why readers are tempted to equate the "destructive element" with life, action, and so on, and the air with ideal illusion. But the passage, which is prefaced by a reference to the "dream" as the dream of what we would like to be, doesn't say that. The dream is equated with the ideal of self or ego-ideal *and* with the sea *and* with the destructive element:

"A man that is born falls into a dream like a man who falls into the sea. If he tries to climb out into the air as inexperienced people endeavour to do, he drowns—*nicht wahr?* . . . No! I tell you! The way is to the destructive element submit yourself, and with the exertions of your hands and feet in the water make the deep, deep sea keep you up." (Chapter XX)

Or: *A man is born ready to create an idealized conception of self, an ego-ideal. If he tries to escape or transcend this conception of self, he collapses. He should accept this ideal and try through action to make it "viable."* (Which is very far from the frequent reading: *man must learn to live with his unideal limitations.*)

But this has become a very dark saying—not only because we think of the ideal as something that transcends, of the ideal as higher, of air as more illusory than water, but also because we think of those who submit to the ego-ideal as "inexperienced" and of those who try to correct it as "experienced." The passage turns out to say something very different from what it appeared to say. There are several possibilities here, including one seldom considered in discussions of famous passages: that Conrad produced without much effort a logically imperfect multiple metaphor, liked the sound of it, and let matters go at that. There is also the possibility that Conrad wanted to show Stein giving confused advice. And there is the very real possibility that Conrad made less distinction between "ego" and "ego-ideal" than we are now accustomed to make. (If the "dream" is equated with "ego" we have less trouble with the climbing into air.) But whether we begin with the ego or with the ideal which, having originated in the ego, carries its own destruction within it, we can probably ascribe to Conrad the pessimism he ascribes to Anatole France:

> He knows that our best hopes are irrealisable; that it is the almost incredible misfortune of mankind, but also its highest privilege, to aspire towards the impossible; that men have never failed to defeat their highest aims by the very strength of their humanity which can conceive the most gigantic tasks but leaves them disarmed before their irremediable littleness. (*Notes on Life and Letters*, p. 33)

Lord Jim has its great structural innovations and successes. What shall we say of its alleged formal weakness: its apparent break into two separate novels, with the second one inferior to the first? A division into two parts certainly exists: the first concerned with Jim's introspective response to the *Patna* incident, the second with the adventurous "second chance" in Patusan. "You've put your finger on the plague spot," Conrad wrote to Garnett concerning this division. A story of continuing distress or slow deterioration might have been more symmetrical. But the very echoing of the crucial names—*Patna, Patusan*—suggests why we must have that second part. The most remote place and unrelated circumstance discovers, in us, the character with which we set out. "A clean slate, did he say? As if the initial word of each our destiny were not graven in imperishable characters upon the face of a rock." There is an aesthetic reason for the Patusan chapters fully as compelling: that by Chapter XVII a story of passive suffering (though the subject was by no means exhausted) threatened to exhaust the reader. Some outlet in action, or at least the illusion of such an oulet, had become necessary. And it is in fact astonishing to see, as we look back, how little has happened in those seventeen chapters in a fictional present time. We have had Jim's gestures as he talks; Marlow and Jim have had their misunderstanding over "cur";

Marlow has had his conversations with Chester and Brierly and Jim has refused Brierly's offer; Marlow has pressed upon him a letter of recommendation. And that is about all.

At the end of Chapter XVII Jim sets out with renewed confidence; his last words are "clean slate." Chapters XVIII–XX may be regarded as transitional: the first two on Jim's retreat "in good order towards the rising sun," as he throws up various jobs; the third on the famous interview with Stein, who sends Jim to Patusan. The second part of the novel would then begin with Chapter XXI, or at the latest with Chapter XXII and Marlow's forestatement of Jim's initial success in Patusan. And its surface material is that of military and political adventure in a remote exotic setting. We may further divide this "second part" in two. Chapters XXII–XXXV deal with the period of Jim's success and carry us to the end of Marlow's original narrative. Chapters XXXVI–XLV deal with the Gentleman Brown incident and Jim's ruin.

It would be pedantic to attach much importance to the fact that *Lord Jim* divides into parts (most novels of its length do) or to be seriously concerned about the shocks of transition. For these shocks are slight, and are not to be blamed on Patusan. The major break comes not with the introduction of the Patusan material (Chapters XXI, XXII) but with the end of Marlow's oral narrative (Chapter XXXV). The important question is whether the novel and its reader are violated in a serious way: either because the material of the second half contradicts the material of the first and devalues it, or because Conrad imagined this material less well, or because it is intrinsically less interesting, or because it demands from us an entirely different kind of attention. Is there, that is, any damaging change in the delicate relationship of author-material-reader?

These questions must be asked, more specifically, of Chapters XXII–XXXV. For this section of the novel, exciting enough at a first reading, does not bear much rereading. The later chapters (XXXVI–XLV), though "adventurous" and "romantic," are very moving; they recover the *authenticity in depth* of the first part. There, once again we are watching character in action; not luck but destiny. And I think this points to the serious weakness of Chapters XXII–XXXV: that the adventures—the wearisome matter of getting the guns up the hill, for instance—have nothing to do with the essential Jim. Hence Conrad (who is less interested in or less convinced by this other Jim) gives a disproportionate attention to the Patusan background. Or can we say —following upon Gordan's demonstration that this successful Jim was based to some degree on James Brooke of Sarawak—that Conrad was here too bemused by his sources? For a while the appalling success of the historic Brooke must have made Jim's introspections seem unimportant; the physical perils are emphasized, not the perils of soul. Marlow now and then steps in to remind us that all this fed Jim's romantic egoism, these successes and physical dangers overcome. But for pages on end the reader is allowed to forget this moral problem and theme. We may add that a characteristic mediocrity sets in with the introduction of Jewel in Chapter XXVIII: with women and their frightening "extra-terrestrial touch," the second standard ingredient of exotic romance. But Chapters XXV–XXVII (on the defeat of Sherif Ali) seem the weakest of all on later readings.

The technical problem for Conrad, at this point in the novel, was a grave one. Only a continuation of the impressionistic method, he must have reasoned, could bridge the gap between the two parts: cover not only the separation of Marlow from Jim and the passage of time, but also the sharp change from passive suffering to adventurous action. Perhaps the reader, caught in the old familiar web and involuted structure, would not try to escape? The reasoning was sound enough, so far as it went. Yet the impressionistic method is one real source of our irritation with Chapters XXV–XXVII, since it has no intrinsic justification. For the method is designed to evoke complex, wavering, suspended responses to infinitely debatable psycho-moral questions; the intricacies and evasions are justified by the fullness of human involvement. But there is little in the three chapters to warrant such reader involvement. They deal with nothing more ambiguous than practical maneuvers: a military action that did or did not succeed.

But this must not be exaggerated. In a novel of great and subtle artistry this structural flaw is one of the few aesthetic facts easy to detect and isolate, hence easy to overemphasize. There is, for instance, no collapse in style as we move into the Patusan material, only a very slight change to suggest that Conrad's creative relationship to the story has changed. With Chapter XXXVII Marlow begins to *write,* though nominally for only one reader: the "privileged man." But a slight significant change to a more written style had already occurred in Chapters XXI and XXII. It suggests that (as Marlow loses his intimate touch with *listeners*) Conrad's own attitude becomes more detached. The style in Chapter XXI now and then approaches that of *The Mirror of the Sea:* "We wander in our thousands over the face of the earth, the illustrious and the obscure, earning beyond the seas our fame, our money, or only a crust of bread; but it seems to me that for each of us going home must be like going to render an account." The distinction between one style and another is a rather delicate one, especially since the speaking Marlow possesses the richness and variety of a written style and the writing Marlow preserves the best qualities of voice. The first of the following passages, though elaborate, keeps the illusion of a man speaking aloud to men; the second, though it has a quality of voice, is essentially "written." The difference comes, among other things, from a higher degree of abstraction in the second passage. There is more of a "novelistic" impulse in the first, no doubt, but both are well done:

"But she turned her back on them as if in disdain of their fate: she had swung round, burdened, to glare stubbornly at the new danger of the open sea which she so strangely survived to end her days in a breaking-up yard, as if it had been her recorded fate to die obscurely under the blows of many hammers. What were the various ends their destiny provided for the pilgrims I am unable to say; but the immediate future brought, at about nine o'clock next morning, a French gunboat homeward bound from Réunion." (Chapter XII)

"It seems impossible to believe that mere greed could hold men to such a steadfastness of purpose, to such a blind persistence in endeavour and sacrifice. And indeed those who adventured their persons and lives risked all they had for a slender reward. They left their bones to lie bleaching on distant shores, so that wealth might flow to the living at home. To us, their less tried successors, they appear magnified, not as agents of trade but as instruments of a recorded destiny, pushing out into the unknown in obedience to an inward voice, to an impulse beating in the blood, to a dream of the future." (Chapter XXII)

The second passage, frankly expository and transitional, is not of course typical of the later chapters. But it does suggest the greater distance or at least altered angle from which Conrad now looked at his story. The solitary white man adventuring into the interior, there to traffic with the natives and become their virtual ruler, and who is presently possessed by what he possesses—such a figure had fascinated Conrad from the first. At the two extremes of fortune might be the Georges Antoine Klein, or Kurtz, who died on board the *Roi des Belges* and the James Brooke who became Rajah of Sarawak, founding a dynasty which lasted until very recently, and one of the world's great fortunes. Both—together with an officer of the *Jeddah* who was not fast enough to get away with the others and so stumbled into undeserved heroism, and together with the braggart Jim Lingard whom Conrad had met—may have gone into the dreaming of *Lord Jim*.[4] But Conrad could dream failure more easily than he could dream success. He could imagine magnificently the failure of Kurtz (when he broke away from *Lord Jim* to write "Heart of Darkness").

[4] John D. Gordon, *Joseph Conrad: The Making of a Novelist* (Cambridge, Mass., 1941), pp. 57–73.

And he could imagine magnificently Jim's failure and death. What he could not imagine, at the same level of intensity and belief, was Jim's period of success.

Discussions of *Lord Jim*, concerned as they are with interpretative and structural problems, regularly neglect the purely novelistic side of vivid particular creation. Mine has been no exception. Yet without the particulars of place and person, without the finely evoked atmospheres and brilliant minor vignettes, the novel's amount of brooding debate might have become intolerable. Its pleasures in any event would have been different ones. Page by page, *Lord Jim's* consistent great appeal largely depends on its changing of the lens, on its sudden shifts from a distant and often nebulous moral perspective to a grossly and superbly material foreground. Marlow's tendency to make such shifts is his most personal and most useful mannerism. It lends reality to the unsubstantial reveries, as gross substance is bound to do, yet invites us to look at them more critically. But most of all it offers the pleasure of a creative surprise. Thus (to take a fine example of sudden rescue from the vague and vast) Cornelius interrupts Marlow's revery, which once again has indulged its fondness for the old problem of "illusion":

"... I have that feeling about me now; perhaps it is that feeling which has incited me to tell you the story, to try to hand over to you, as it were, its very existence, its reality—the truth disclosed in a moment of illusion.

"Cornelius broke upon it. He bolted out, vermin-like, from the long grass growing in a depression of the ground. I believe his house was rotting somewhere near by, though I've never seen it, not having been far enough in that direction. He ran towards me upon the path; his feet, shod in dirty white shoes, twinkled on the dark earth: he pulled himself up, and began to whine and cringe under a tall stovepipe hat. His dried-up little carcass was swallowed up, totally lost, in a suit of black broadcloth." (Chapter XXXIV)

Conrad's success with such minor figures is (as we look back on the earlier work and forward to *Nostromo*) one of the substantial advances registered by *Lord Jim*. Cornelius, Marlow remarks, merely skulks on the "outskirts" of the story. But the account of his trembling attempt to get rid of Jim is fine dramatic writing. Through a slight narrative distance (we are never told in so many words what Cornelius intends) we watch him try to sell Jim protection for eighty dollars, then hover outside the house in the darkness, apparently waiting to see him killed. We know his intentions by his behavior when Jim appears unexpectedly: the way he ducks sideways as though shot at, his panic

as he clings to the rail of the verandah, his "faint shriek" when Jim
appears again.

Criticism, it may be, pays too little attention to the vivid minor
figure, and to the pleasure and actualizing effect of surprise. *Lord Jim*
obviously depends very heavily on intellectual surprise, as the reader
is compelled to make large and sudden adjustments and resolve conflicting demands. But the lesser surprises are important too. The
German captain of the *Patna*, for instance, reaches us through a series
of surprises. He is created by them. He is dramatically introduced,
after a long elevated passage on the pilgrims coming aboard the *Patna*,
by his brief remark: "Look at dese cattle . . ." And a surprise may
be most effective when it proves to be true in an unexpected way. The
fanciful metaphor to convey his voice has its exactness: "From the
thick throat of the commander of the *Patna* came a low rumble, on
which the sound of the word *schwein* fluttered high and low like a
capricious feather in a faint stir of air." Presently we see him (who also
is being taken "unawares") slide into the harbor office and Archie
Ruthvel's presence: "something round and enormous, resembling a
sixteen-hundred-weight sugar-hogshead wrapped in striped flannelette,
up-ended in the middle of the large floor space." And finally we see
him drive off in the gharry to the astonishment of his subordinates,
the monstrous fatness somehow squeezed into that "little box on
wheels":

> ". . . but it only sank with a click of flattened springs, and suddenly one
> venetian blind rattled down. His shoulders reappeared, jammed in the
> small opening; his head hung out, distended and tossing like a captive
> balloon, perspiring, furious, spluttering. He reached for the gharry-wallah
> with vicious flourishes of a fist as dumpy and red as a lump of raw meat.
> He roared at him to be off, to go on. Where? Into the Pacific, perhaps.
> The driver lashed; the pony snorted, reared once, and darted off at a
> gallop. Where? To Apia? to Honolulu? He had 6,000 miles of tropical
> belt to disport himself in, and I did not hear the precise address. A snort-
> ing pony snatched him into 'ewigkeit' in the twinkling of an eye, and I
> never saw him again. . . ." (Chapter V)

A connected account of *Lord Jim* (unless it is to rival the novel in
length) is bound to neglect such fine particulars. Thus a discussion of
Chapter XIV must mention Jim's loss of his certificate and the
cynicism of Chester's offer. But our living experience of the chapter is
no little affected by the plaintiff in the assault case: "an obese choco-
late-coloured man with shaved head, one fat breast bare and a bright
yellow caste-mark above the bridge of his nose, sat in pompous immobility: only his eyes glittered, rolling in the gloom, and the nostrils
dilated and collapsed violently as he breathed." It is affected infinitely

more, of course, by the brief portrait of Captain Robinson, who had once been reduced to cannibalism. Chester's story is made vivid in classical fictional ways:

" . . . a boat of Her Majesty's ship *Wolverine* found [Robinson] kneeling on the kelp, naked as the day he was born, and chanting some psalm-tune or other; light snow was falling at the time. He waited till the boat was an oar's length from the shore, and then up and away. They chased him for an hour up and down the boulders, till a marine flung a stone that took him behind the ear providentially and knocked him senseless. Alone? Of course. . . ." (Chapter XIV)

This is fine enough, and credible enough. But the great fictional stroke was to interrupt Chester's talk with the appearance of Captain Robinson himself, a doddering and "amiable" old man:

"An emaciated patriarch in a suit of white drill, a solar topi with a green-lined rim on a head trembling with age, joined us after cross-ing the street in a trotting shuffle, and stood propped with both hands on the handle of an umbrella. A white beard with amber streaks hung lumpily down to his waist. He blinked his creased eyelids at me in a bewildered way. 'How do you do? how do you do?' he piped, amiably, and tottered. 'A little deaf,' said Chester aside." (Chapter XIV)

The naked chanting Robinson and the Robinson with amber-streaked white beard, the plaintiff with his one fat breast bare and eyes rolling in the gloom, the monstrously fat captain of the *Patna* and the monstrously fat Doramin, the slinking Cornelius and his twinkling white shoes, Gentleman Brown and the "sunken glare of his fierce crow-footed eyes"—all alike remind us of the old paradox: that the successfully achieved grotesque has a kind of fictional reality that the flat and commonplace seldom attains. Conrad will show even more of this novelistic creativity, this intense visual and dramatic surprise, in *Nostromo.*

PART TWO

View Points

Joseph Conrad: Letter to John Galsworthy

Pent Farm
Friday [about July 20th, 1900]

Dearest Jack,

. . . The end of *L.J.* [*Lord Jim.* The writing of the novel had been finished on the 16th.] has been pulled off with a steady drag of 21 hours. I sent wife and child out of the house (to London) and sat down at 9 A.M. with a desperate resolve to be done with it. Now and then I took a walk round the house, out one door in at the other. Ten-minute meals. A great hush. Cigarette ends growing into a mound similar to a cairn over a dead hero. Moon rose over the barn, looked in at the window and climbed out of sight. Dawn broke, brightened. I put the lamp out and went on, with the morning breeze blowing the sheets of MS. all over the room. Sun rose. I wrote the last word and went into the dining-room. Six o'clock I shared a piece of cold chicken with Escamillo [Conrad's dog] (who was very miserable and in want of sympathy, having missed the child dreadfully all day). Felt very well, only sleepy: had a bath at seven and at 1:30 was on my way to London. . . .

Joseph Conrad: Letter to Edward Garnett

Pent Farm
12 Nov. 1900

Dearest E.,

You are great and good.

Yes! You've put your finger on the plague spot. The division of the book [*Lord Jim*] into two parts, which is the basis of your criticism, demonstrates to me once more your amazing insight; and your analysis

This and the following letter are from G. *Jean-Aubry,* Joseph Conrad: Life and Letters *(New York: Doubleday & Company, Inc., 1927), I, 295–96 and 298–99; Copyright 1926, 1927 by Doubleday & Company, Inc. Reprinted by permission of J. M. Dent & Sons Ltd. and the Trustees of the Joseph Conrad Estate.*

of the effect of the book puts into words precisely and suggestively the dumb thoughts of every reader—and my own.

Such is indeed the effect of the book; the effect which you can name and others can only feel. I admit I stood for a great triumph and I have only succeeded in giving myself utterly away. Nobody'll see it, but you have detected me falling back into my lump of clay I had been lugging up from the bottom of the pit, with the idea of breathing big life into it. And all I have done was to let it fall with a silly crash. For what is fundamentally wrong with the book—the cause and the effect—is want of power. I do not mean the "power" of reviewers' jargon. I mean the want of illuminating imagination. I wanted to obtain a sort of lurid light out [of] the very events. You know what I have done—alas! I haven't been strong enough to breathe the right sort of life into my clay—the *revealing* life.

I've been satanically ambitious, but there's nothing of a devil in me, worse luck. The *Outcast* is a heap of sand, the *Nigger* a splash of water, *Jim* a lump of clay. A stone, I suppose, will be my next gift to impatient mankind—before I get drowned in mud to which even my supreme struggles won't give a simulacrum of life. Poor mankind! Drop a tear for it—but look how infinitely more pathetic I am! This pathos is a kind of triumph no criticism can touch. Like the philosopher who crowed at the Universe, I shall know when I am utterly squashed. This time I am only very bruised, very sore, very humiliated.

This is the effect of the book upon me; the intimate and personal effect. Humiliation. Not extinction. Not yet. All of you stand by me so nobly that I must still exist. There is *You*, always, and never dismayed. I had an amazing note from Lucas. Amazing! This morning a letter came from Henry James.[1] Ah! You rub in the balm till every sore smarts—therefore I exist. The time will come when you shall get tired of tending a true and most well-intentioned sham—and then the end'll come too.

But keep up! Keep up! Let me exhort you earnestly to keep up! as long as you can.

I send you the H. J. [Henry James] letter. A draught from the Fountain of Eternal Youth. Wouldn't you think a boy had written it? Such enthusiasm! Wonderful old man, with his record of wonderful work! It is, I believe seriously intended (the letter) as confidential. And to you alone I show it—keep *his* secret for us both. No more now. I've read *Petersburg Tales* [by Olive Garnett]. Phew! That *is* something! That is many things—and the only thing—it is written! It is. That work is genuine, undeniable, constructed and inhabited. It has founda-

---

[1] This letter has been lost—ed.

tion and life. I hope the writer will deign to recognize my most fraternal welcome!

P.S. Pray send the James autograph back—registered. Our great love to you three. We *must* meet soon.

Joseph Conrad: Author's Note to *Lord Jim*

When this novel first appeared in book form a notion got about that I had been bolted away with. Some reviewers maintained that the work starting as a short story had got beyond the writer's control. One or two discovered internal evidence of the fact, which seemed to amuse them. They pointed out the limitations of the narrative form. They argued that no man could have been expected to talk all that time, and other men to listen so long. It was not, they said, very credible.

After thinking it over for something like sixteen years I am not so sure about that. Men have been known, both in the tropics and in the temperate zone, to sit up half the night "swapping yarns." This, how-ever, is but one yarn, yet with interruptions affording some measure of relief; and in regard to the listeners' endurance, the postulate must be accepted that the story *was* interesting. It is the necessary prelimi-nary assumption. If I hadn't believed that it *was* interesting I could never have begun to write it. As to the mere physical possibility we all know that some speeches in Parliament have taken nearer six than three hours in delivery; whereas all that part of the book which is Marlow's narrative can be read through aloud, I should say, in less than three hours. Besides—though I have kept strictly all such in-significant details out of the tale—we may presume that there must have been refreshments on that night, a glass of mineral water of some sort to help the narrator on.

But, seriously, the truth of the matter is, that my first thought was of a short story, concerned only with the pilgrim ship episode; nothing more. And that was a legitimate conception. After writing a few pages, however, I became for some reason discontented and I laid them aside for a time. I didn't take them out of the drawer till the late Mr. William Blackwood suggested I should give something again to his magazine.

It was only then that I perceived that the pilgrim ship episode was a good starting-point for a free and wandering tale; that it was an event, too, which could conceivably colour the whole "sentiment of

Joseph Conrad, Author's Note to Lord Jim *(London: J. M. Dent and Sons, Ltd.). Reprinted by permission of the publisher and the Trustees of the Joseph Conrad Estate.*

existence" in a simple and sensitive character. But all these prelimi-
nary moods and stirrings of spirit were rather obscure at the time, and
they do not appear clearer to me now after the lapse of so many years.

The few pages I had laid aside were not without their weight in the
choice of subject. But the whole was re-written deliberately. When I
sat down to it I knew it would be a long book, though I didn't foresee
that it would spread itself over thirteen numbers of "Maga."

I have been asked at times whether this was not the book of mine
I liked best. I am a great foe to favouritism in public life, in private
life, and even in the delicate relationship of an author to his works.
As a matter of principle I will have no favourites; but I don't go so
far as to feel grieved and annoyed by the preference some people give
to my Lord Jim. I won't even say that I "fail to understand. . . ." No!
But once I had occasion to be puzzled and surprised.

A friend of mine returning from Italy had talked with a lady there
who did not like the book. I regretted that, of course, but what surprised me was the ground of her dislike. "You know," she said, "it is all
so morbid."

The pronouncement gave me food for an hour's anxious thought.
Finally I arrived at the conclusion that, making due allowances for
the subject itself being rather foreign to women's normal sensibilities,
the lady could not have been an Italian. I wonder whether she was
European at all? In any case, no Latin temperament would have perceived anything morbid in the acute consciousness of lost honour. Such
a consciousness may be wrong, or it may be right, or it may be condemned as artificial; and, perhaps, my Jim is not a type of wide com-
monness. But I can safely assure my readers that he is not the product
of coldly perverted thinking. He's not a figure of Northern Mists
either. One sunny morning in the commonplace surroundings of an
Eastern roadstead, I saw his form pass by—appealing—significant—
under a cloud—perfectly silent. Which is as it should be. It was for
me, with all the sympathy of which I was capable, to seek fit words for
his meaning. He was "one of us."

June, 1917.   J.C.

David Daiches

Lord Jim (1900) has certain weaknesses resulting largely from the
fact that it was originally conceived as a short story (dealing only with

David Daiches, The Novel and The Modern World, Revised Edition (Chicago:
University of Chicago Press, 1960), pp. 31–36. Copyright © 1960 by the University
of Chicago. Reprinted by permission of the publisher and the author.

the "Patna" incident) and was later elaborated, with the well-known shifts in point of view and manipulations of time-sequence, into a complex exploration—of problems of guilt, pride, self-deception, and related moral ambiguities—that reveals much that is central in Conrad's attitude and technique. Marlow, who tells much of Jim's story, reveals by his hesitations and questionings his own uncertainty about the meaning of it all. The central situation is itself ambiguous. Jim, the imaginative and accomplished young first mate of the "Patna" who allowed himself to be persuaded by the skipper and others to leave what he considered the doomed ship with the crew and passengers sleeping on board and has his mate's certificate revoked by the court of inquiry in consequence, is the only one of the three guilty men who remains to face the music, to attend the inquiry, to hear his sentence. He is better than the other two; if, under circumstances that he cannot properly explain even to himself, he allowed himself to jump from the doomed ship, he nevertheless is convinced that there were some special, strange, indefinable extenuating circumstances which mitigate his guilt and account for everything. This is a kind of self-deception, clearly. But is his remaining to face the inquiry a sign of grace or a sign of false romanticism? Is he as different from the other two guilty men as he imagines? Is he really running away when he thinks he is facing it out? He gets a job as a water clerk, but as soon as somebody arrives in the port who knows about the "Patna" Jim throws up his job and moves further eastward, and so he moves further and further away from the outposts of Western civilization until he reaches his final haven and his final test in Patusan: is this courage or cowardice—or a bewildering mixture of both? Jim will not face the truth about himself; he insists on regarding his past as a cruel accident. He wants to undo it by some heroic gesture, some ideal achievement. The position he makes for himself in Patusan, as savior and protector of a native community, is in some respects an ideal achievement, yet it is at the same time an escape and an excuse. He betrays his people—unintentionally—to Gentleman Brown because he accepts the blackmail of identification between Brown and himself, insinuated by Brown, and then makes amends to *himself* by going to his certain and useless death in a gesture of purely romantic histrionics. Is this his ultimate vindication or his ultimate failure? He goes to his death against the entreaties of the devoted Jewel, replying to her protests with the announcement that "Nothing can touch me"—said "in a last flicker of superb egotism."

Whose diagnosis is the right one? Marlow himself cannot be sure. The French naval lieutenant is unable to give an opinion on what life may be worth when honor is gone. The benevolent and wise Mr. Stein, who is the means of giving Jim the opportunity to redeem himself in Patusan—if it is really a redemption—explains that Jim "is romantic —romantic. . . . And that is very bad." He has his own prescription. "A man that is born falls into a dream like a man who falls into the sea. If he tries to climb out into the air as inexperienced people endeavor to do, he drowns. . . . The way is to the destructive element submit yourself, and with the exertions of your hands and feet in the water make the deep, deep sea keep you up. . . . In the destructive element immerse." But Stein himself is a romantic German, and the conversation with Marlow in which he gives this prescription in the dusk of an eastern night is curiously self-indulgent. In any case, his advice is ambiguous. Does it mean that a man must not try to escape from his dream into the world of reality for that will kill him? If it means this, is he not preaching living in an unreal world? In a sense, was not that what Jim had been doing in refusing to admit that he had failed the test and seeking always for an explanation and a way of vindication? Stein and his destructive element are themselves parts of the puzzle, not Conrad's solution.

Lord Jim is not a study of a romantic young man redeeming a terrible moment of cowardice by later bravery and self-sacrifice, nor is it a study of a weak young man whose vanity makes him unable to come to terms with his weakness. Yet each of these descriptions is in some sense and in some degree true. Jim's final act of surrendering his life is heroic, though it is also exhibitionist and useless. And in a sense his failure on the "Patna" was not a straightforward act of betrayal or cowardice. The cause was partly his too lively imagination— and imagination, we must remember, is the sympathetic faculty which destroyed the morale of the crew of the "Narcissus." Jim visualized with great clarity what would happen if the packed body of sleeping pilgrims were to be awakened to a sense of their inevitable doom (as Jim considered it); he saw in his own lively mind the panic and horror; and as a result he allowed himself to believe that it would be best for all concerned if they sank quietly and asleep with the ship. But the ship didn't sink, and Jim's decision became in cold, objective fact, a gross dereliction of duty. Jim will never admit that it was a decision; it was something that happened to him. When explaining the events of that night to Marlow, he tells of how the others had got into the boat and then eventually "I had jumped. . . . It seems." He insists to Marlow that he was prepared "for all the difficulties that can beset one on land and water." "He had been rehearsing dangers and defences, expecting the worst, rehearsing his best." What actually happened fitted in to none of his rehearsals. When Marlow remarks, "It is always the unexpected that happens," Jim brushes the remark aside.

Yet he might have known. We are shown a preview of the "Patna" disaster in the opening chapter, when Jim delays in joining the rescue party from the training-ship and finds suddenly that he is too late, has lost his opportunity. We are told also in Chapter II that Jim became chief mate "when yet very young, . . . without ever having been tested by those events of the sea that show in the light of day the inner worth of a man, the edge of his temper, and the fibre of his stuff; that reveal the quality of his resistance and the secret truth of his pretences, not only to others but also to himself." Jim never learned "the secret truth of his pretences." Were his pretenses vindicated in the end? The answer remains ambiguous. But one of his moral deficiencies was that he was unable to cope with the secret sharer.

There is another character in *Lord Jim* who cannot cope with the secret sharer: that is Captain Brierly, one of the assessors at the inquiry. Enormously successful in his maritime career, envied by all, Brierly yet has a secret sense of guilt which is revealed to him as he listens to the facts of Jim's case. Less than a week after the inquiry he commits suicide by jumping over the side of his ship. The incident is not fully realized in the story and it is left deliberately mysterious. But Conrad leaves us in no doubt that Brierly sees himself as Jim, for reasons and in a manner unrevealed to us, and the recognition compels his suicide. "Who can tell what flattering view he had induced himself to take of his own suicide?" asks Marlow, and the question could even more appropriately be asked of Jim, whose final death is really a form of suicide.

The Patusan scenes in *Lord Jim* are the least satisfactory, and Jim's establishment of himself as the father of a Malay community is altogether too facilely presented. Yet the novel survives it. The questionings and ambiguities of Marlow's narrative and the shifts of focus provided by Conrad in the unfolding of the story succeed in giving it the dimensions he requires for it. If you cannot be simple-minded and unimaginative like Captain MacWhirr of *Typhoon*, you are likely to find your good qualities warring against each other. Sensitivity, imagination, sympathy—they all can corrupt, either by encouraging self-deception or in other ways. And pride, which is necessary if a man is to have confidence in himself and his code (it is significant that the evil skipper of the "Patna" has no pride at all), can also produce self-flattering illusions and escapist exhibitionism. The code we live by may be all right for the ordinary man or the ordinary moment, but if when the testing point comes either the man has too much imagination or the moment is of a wholly unanticipated kind, the code is challenged with disturbing results. To face the wholly unanticipated successfully requires either stolidness or high qualities

that transcend imagination and smpathy. Jim falls between the alternatives. He is not wholly guilty, we cannot help feeling, for the effect of
that "I had jumped. . . . It seems" is to make the reader share Jim's
sense of disbelief in his own guilt. Yet the reader is aware at the same
time that he ought not to share this disbelief. The measure of the
success of this unequal novel lies in the degree to which Conrad's
method of narration has involved the reader in this way.

Robert B. Heilman

Lord Jim, in all its remarkableness, is hardly explicable as the product of Conrad's literary experience and taste and his forebears. He
preferred Turgenev to Dostoevski and in fiction in English had some
fondness for Cooper and Marryat. A long admiration for Dickens,
whose influence on Conrad is discussed by F. R. Leavis in *The Great
Tradition,* perhaps reflects itself in certain comic elements in *Lord Jim*
that have a Dickensian flavor—the affected style of Brierly's successor
on the *Ossa* (Chapter VI), the grotesque comedy of the terrified officers
on the *Patna* (Chapter IX), Sigmund Yucker's dyspepsia, recounted in
broken English (Chapter XIX), Stein's ship captain's fancy language
(Chapter XXIII), the grotesqueness of Jim's muddy state when he
escapes to Doramin (Chapter XXV), the description of Doramin
(Chapter XXVI). In the direct application of philosophical awareness
to the materials of fiction he has same rough affiliations with George
Eliot, Meredith, and Hardy, but in contrast with at least the latter
two Conrad is much less likely to bog down in topicalities—science,
the state of society, conventions, the church, and so on. He might be
thought of as continuing from Eliot: both are concerned with the
underside of the success story, the drift into guilt, the regenerating
act; both have that profound consciousness of man's dual potentiality
—his ability to damn himself and to save himself—that is essential to
the writing of the tragic novel (when the consciousness of man's
doubleness is lost, we get the literature of despair and disaster on one
side, and of sentimental optimism on the other—both rather familiar
in fiction). Yet Conrad's range is greater than Eliot's. Part of his
greatness is his wide sense of good and evil. His spectrum of evil includes the bald nastiness of the *Patna* captain, the cringing and whin-
ing treacherousness of Cornelius, the soulless scheming of Chester

Robert B. Heilman, from "Introduction to Lord Jim" *(New York: Holt, Rinehart
and Winston, 1957). Copyright © 1957 by Robert B. Heilman. Reprinted by permission of the author.*

(who, as the man outside the "dream," prescribes, "You must see things as they are"—Chapter XIV), and above all the merciless virulent destructiveness of Gentleman Brown—the Lucifer type of villain (who after his fall from "high place" becomes the intellectual and moral leader of a predatory mob and whom Conrad, as if fascinated, explores again in Mr. Jones of *Victory*). These human horrors Conrad can imagine wonderfully and yet limit them to a peripheral role in order to save the center of the stage for the conflict of good and evil in Jim. For Jim is that rare creature in English fiction—the tragic hero. He is, as Stein says, certainly "good"—"What is it that by inward pain makes him know himself? What is it that for you and me makes him—exist?" The good man must come to terms with what we have called ugly surprises from within—the realm of human danger that Conrad, as tragic writer, is more concerned with than with the deeds of all the men wholly committed to evil. Jim's flaw could lead to disintegration, but Conrad sees him as capable of finding the spiritual salvation which, in the tradition of high tragedy, transcends the catastrophe of events. Jim has to go through the tragic course of knowing himself and thus learning the way to salvation, for, like many a tragic hero, he tries at first to live in a melodrama where what is wrong is in others and in circumstances. "Was ever there any one so shamefully tried!" is his early complaint (Chapter IX).

Finally there is the range of Jim himself, who is a very inclusive character. In him is the universal skeleton in the closet; not the heroic pride that would leap over all common bounds (Faust, Macbeth), but that defect in the heroic which makes him slip out of common bonds. In him we see generic man as he is endowed with the "romantic" imagination that may open a pit under him or supply him with the grace to earn the heroic; the man whose failure makes all sentient men worry profoundly (Marlow) or despair (Brierly). As we read his story we sense its affiliations with other stories and even with genres of story. Jim may seem at first an unlikely double of Othello, yet their lives have a common pattern: they give up for lost what is not lost, and a sense of self pries them away from faith and obligation. To go even further in finding likeness at the heart of apparent unlikeness: on the one hand, Jim's story is a version of the modern "success story"; on the other, of the ancient myth of Oedipus (Dorothy Van Ghent discusses at length the relevance of the Oedipus myth and other classical myths). Jim is the prototype of the boy who "makes good," but what Conrad does is to explode the popular stereotype by ultimately defining the "good" in qualitative and spiritual instead of quantitative terms. We find, on inspection, that the success story is not entirely alien to the Oedipus myth. For Oedipus, too, has "Ability in the abstract"; he has the talent

for saving a distressed community, as Jim has. Jim's "success" comes
after he has sought to escape the truth by moving from port to port,
just as Oedipus has sought to evade destiny by a change of scene—both
versions of the common myth of "leaving town." When at last there is
nowhere else to retreat to, they discover their deepest talents; for both
the ultimate deed is a paradox, success-in-failure.

Lord Jim, of course, must be judged in terms of its own form, but
such parallels as these may help suggest the magnitude of Conrad's
achievement. One of the ironies of authorship is Conrad's own low
opinion of this fine work just after he had finished it. On November
12, 1900, he wrote sadly to Edward Garnett: "For what is fundamentally wrong with the book—the cause and effect—is want of power. I
do not mean the 'power' of reviewers' jargon. I mean the want of illuminating imagination."

Douglas Hewitt

The effect of muddlement which is so commonly found in *Lord Jim*
comes, in short, from this—that Marlow is himself muddled. We look
to him for a definite comment, explicit or implicit, on Jim's conduct
and he is not able to give it. We are inevitably reminded of the bewilderment with which the Marlow of "Heart of Darkness" faces
Kurtz. By appealing to "that side of us which, like the other hemisphere of the moon, exists stealthily in perpetual darkness" he confronts
Marlow with "issues beyond the competency of a court of inquiry"
and thus shakes the standards by which he would normally be judged.

Here, as in the short story, the experience of Marlow goes far beyond
that of the man whom he cannot disown. Kurtz is only a "hollow
man," Jim himself is, by comparison with Marlow, naïve, a romantic thinking in the terms of a boy's adventure story.

But the muddlement goes farther than this. I have so far begged the
question by saying "Marlow, Conrad's mouthpiece." In fact the confusion seems to extend to Conrad's conception of the story, and this
reveals itself in some of the rhetoric given to Marlow. A good deal of
this is imprecise and some is little more than a vague and rather pre-
tentious playing with abstractions. It is in these terms that he speaks
of the approaching catastrophe:

> *Magna est veritas et* . . . Yes, when it gets a chance. There is a law,
> no doubt—and likewise a law regulates your luck in the throwing of

Douglas Hewitt, Conrad: A Reassessment *(Cambridge: Bowes and Bowes, 1952),*
pp. 37–39. Reprinted by permission of the publisher.

dice. It is not Justice, the servant of men, but accident, hazard, Fortune
—the ally of patient Time—that holds an even and scrupulous balance
. . . Well, let's leave it to chance, whose ally is Time, that cannot be
hurried, and whose enemy is Death, that will not wait.

There are many such passages, and they give the impression rather of a
man who is ruminating to obscure the issue than of one thinking to
clarify it. But they are not "placed"—Conrad, that is, does not so
present them that we see them as deliberate, part of the portrayal of a
man who is bewildered. They come rather from his own uncertainty as
to the effect at which he is aiming. There is, very clearly, a conflict in
his own mind; he raises the issue of the sufficiency of the "few simple
notions you must cling to if you want to live decently," but he does
not, throughout the book, face it consistently.

Lord Jim is, at bottom, concerned with the same preoccupations as
"Heart of Darkness" and other works of this period, but Conrad has
chosen to treat them in such a way that he inevitably feels more
directly concerned. As he says in the concluding words of the "Author's
Note": "He was 'one of us'." The uncertainty which remains even at
the end of the book as to what judgment we should pass on Jim and the
passages of imprecise rhetoric are, I believe, an indication that his
feelings are too deeply and too personally involved for him to stand
above the bewilderment in which he places Marlow. The fixed standards of the simple sailor are those which, above all others, Conrad
finds it difficult to treat with detachment. He was too aware of the
depths of treachery and cowardice of which men are capable not to
cherish whatever seems to provide a defense against them, and at
times we have the impression that, just as much as Marlow, he is
himself fighting to retain a faith in the efficacy and total goodness
of the "few simple notions."

Frederick Karl

Jim, as we leave him, is a man of self-conceived romance and mis-
placed imagination who is perforce a failure. Suffering as he does from
an excess of imagination, he resembles that greatly-admired hero of
both Conrad and Flaubert, Don Quixote. Conrad called Jim a romantic and perhaps he saw him as Henry James saw Emma Bovary—as of
romantic temper and realistic adventures. Jim is clearly in the line of

Frederick Karl, A Reader's Guide to Joseph Conrad (*New York: Noonday Press,
1960*), *pp. 130–31. Copyright © 1960 by Frederick Karl. Reprinted by permission
of the author.*

those romantic heroes whose awareness of reality never catches up with the roles they have idealized for themselves.

Stein, conversely, suggests reality, control, forethought. His advice that one must immerse in the destructive element—a loose paraphrase of Novalis' "Most men will not swim before they are able to."—conveys his realization of man's limited powers. *Realization* is perhaps the key word in *Lord Jim,* as much as it is the key to tragedy. But only Stein, not Jim, *realizes.* The latter, because he beats against life without ever recognizing his role, will always consider himself a failure—and tragic heroes are made of other stuff. Stein's presence, then, is truly the destructive element, for his multifarious activities—his controlled romanticism, his grasp of reality, for example—allow alternatives to Jim's compulsiveness, and the alternatives, had Jim acted upon them and still failed, would have provided the stuff of real tragedy.

The novel, even if it lacks the tragic sense, still remains, of course, a rich and varied experience. Jim in his semi-articulate and stumbling way, in his sense of almost complete failure, in his inability to act powerfully and wisely, is a compelling guide to the modern temper; and his frustrated quest for personal salvation in an evil world is Conrad's distressing prophecy for the twentieth century. Although *Lord Jim* is more imposing in its parts than as a whole, it nevertheless retains a power and a force rarely duplicated by Conrad's contemporaries or by Conrad himself in his later work; obviously, Conrad's way of conceiving this novel makes *Lord Jim* his as yet most pregnant statement on man. His ability to suggest and evoke is evident, and from here to "Heart of Darkness" is not a great step.

F. R. Leavis

In *Lord Jim* Marlow is the means of presenting Jim with the appropriate externality, seen always through the question, the doubt, that is the central theme of the book. Means and effect are unobjectionable; it is a different matter from the use of Marlow elsewhere to pass off a vaguely excited incomprehension as tremendous significance. But *Lord Jim* doesn't deserve the position of pre-eminence among Conrad's works often assigned it: it is hardly one of the most considerable. There is, in fact, much to be said in support of those reviewers who (Conrad tells us) "maintained that the work starting as a short story

F. R. Leavis, The Great Tradition (*London: Chatto & Windus, Ltd., 1948*), *pp. 189–90. Reprinted by permission of Chatto & Windus, Ltd., and New York University Press.*

had got beyond the writer's control," so that what we have is neither
a very considerable novel, in spite of its 420 pages, nor one of Conrad's
best short stories. The presentment of Lord Jim in the first part of
the book, the account of the inquiry and of the desertion of the *Patna,*
the talk with the French lieutenant—these are good Conrad. But the
romance that follows, though plausibly offered as a continued exhibi-
tion of Jim's case, has no inevitability as that; nor does it develop or
enrich the central interest, which consequently, eked out to provide
the substance of a novel, comes to seem decidedly thin.

The eking out is done mainly from the world of *Almayer's Folly, An
Outcast of the Islands,* and *Tales of Unrest,* those excessively adjectival
studies in the Malayan exotic of Conrad's earliest vein. Those things,
it had better be said here, though they are innocuous, and no doubt
deserved for their originality of setting some respectful notice when
they came out, will not be urged by judicious admirers of Conrad
among his claims to classical rank. In their stylistic eloquence, which
suggests a descent from Chateaubriand, their wearying exoticism, and
their "picturesque" human interest, they aren't easy to re-read. No,
Lord Jim is neither the best of Conrad's novels, nor among the best of
his short stories.

Morton Dauwen Zabel

The dramatic diffusion, the puzzled intelligence, the struggling
movement, the disrupted chronology, the excess of surmise and commentary, the over-insistent paradox—these must be admitted. They
seem as inevitable to the existence of the novel as the vision in which
it originated or the desperate tenacity by which it was pushed to its
conclusion. The question is: could a book like *Lord Jim* have been
written on any other terms? It is easy enough to discount Conrad's
minor tales and later rhetorical dramas. These are obviously the pro-
ducts either of a forced convention or of an exhausted inspiration. But
it is impossible to discount or undervalue *Lord Jim* or the dozen other
novels and tales that share its power. Such works are perhaps by defini-
tion imperfect. They issue from too intimate a source, too personal and
urgent an impulse. They may miss the self-defining quality and controlled vision by which some works of profound originality justify
themselves. But their very imperfection defines the sources of insight,

Morton Dauwen Zabel, from "Introduction to Lord Jim" *(Boston, Mass.: Hough-
ton Mifflin Company, 1958). Copyright © 1958 by Morton Dauwen Zabel. Reprinted
by permission of the publisher.*

ruthless inquisition, and unsparing tenacity out of which they grow. Measured by such qualities, *Lord Jim* is not only a passionate and noble book. It is one of the books that establish the basis of sincerity and moral capacity on which the highest achievement in modern fiction rests.

To read it today is to be reminded anew of how the power of an intensely dramatic and visual imagination may redeem the conflict, complexity, and struggle to which the moral vision of our century is committed. The great scenes of the book tether its perplexity and ambiguity to that saving realism. Its most powerful passages—the voyage of the *Patna,* the scenes at the Inquiry, Marlow's first meeting with Jim, his interview with the French lieutenant, the role of Stein, Marlow's last sight of Jim on the shore of Patusan, the coming of Brown, Jim's final surrender—are scenes not only unforgettable. They show the force and suggestive power that permit them to fly off from the story and take a longer lease on life in the symbolizing imagination. Innumerable smaller details add their effect: the ship striking the sunken hulk, the jump to the lifeboat, the dog in the crowd, the "clear tinkle of a teaspoon falling on the tesselated floor of the verandah," ringing out "like a tiny and silvery scream," the sea breaking on the Patusan coast as against a "sombre wall that seemed the very stronghold of the night." It is these that compel us to hear, feel, and see an experience that may become part of our conscious and unconscious lives. They act to perpetuate in the reader's mind and emotion the ordeal of a soul under test, and compel him to recognize that neither the soul nor the test are fantasies but part of a "visible world," an "invincible truth," and "a common fate" he has come to share. It is by enforcing that recognition that *Lord Jim* stands high among the modern novels that testify to "the reality of our existence," and shows its sincerity in a high ambition. No serious experience of the art of fiction can ignore its value or fail to see it as one of the books of our century that have set a mark and defined a standard.

Chronology of Important Dates

	Conrad	The Age
1857	Dec. 3 Conrad (Josef Tedor Konrad Nalecz Korzeniowski) born in Poland (under Russian rule).	*Madame Bovary.*
1859		*The Origin of the Species.*
1862	C.'s father condemned to exile in Russia for taking part in Polish Nationalist Committee. C. and mother accompany him.	
1865	C.'s mother dies in exile.	Yeats b.; Kipling b.
1866	C. sent to live with uncle, Tadeusz Bobrowski.	*Crime and Punishment.*
1867		*Capital, I.*
1868	C.'s father permitted to live in Galicia. C. attends high school there.	
1869	C.'s father dies. C. continues his education in Cracow.	Suez Canal opened; André Gide b.
1870		Dickens d.; Lenin b.; Franco-Prussian War; Italy unified.
1871		Proust b.
1872	C. announces to his uncle his desire to go to sea.	
1873	C. travels in Europe.	
1875	C. joins French marine service.	Victoria titled Empress of India; *Anna Karenina.*

1876–94	Career at sea.	
1881		*The Portrait of a Lady.*
1882		Joyce b.; Virginia Woolf b.
1885		Lawrence b.
1886	C. naturalized as British subject.	
1889		Browning d.
1892		Tennyson d.
1895	*Almayer's Folly.*	Oscar Wilde scandal; Freud's *Studies of Hysteria.*
1896	C. marries Jessie George. (1898, son Borys b.; 1906, son Alexander b.).	
1897	*The Nigger of the "Narcissus."*	
1899–1902		Boer War.
1900	*Lord Jim.*	*Buddenbrooks.*
1901	*The Inheritors* (with Ford Madox Ford).	Victoria d.
1902		*The Immoralist.*
1904	*Nostromo.*	*The Golden Bowl.*
1905	C. granted Civil List pension for service to literature.	
1906		Ibsen d.
1907	*The Secret Agent.*	
1910		Tolstoy d.
1913		*Sons and Lovers.*
1913–27		*A la Recherche du temps perdu.*
1914	*Chance.*	
1914–18		World War I.
1915	*Victory.*	
1916		James d.

1917	C. writes prefaces to his collected works (1917–20).	Bolshevik Revolution.
1922		*Ulysses; The Waste Land;* Proust d.
1923	C. visits United States.	
1924	C. declines Knighthood. Dies on Aug. 3. Buried at Canterbury.	*The Magic Mountain;* Kafka d.

Notes on the Editor and Contributors

ROBERT E. KUEHN teaches English at Yale where he is also Dean of Jonathan Edwards College.

JOCELYN BAINES is the author of *Joseph Conrad: A Critical Biography.*

DAVID DAICHES is the author of numerous works of literary criticism in addition to *The Novel and the Modern World.* He is Professor of English and Dean of English and American Studies at the University of Sussex.

ALBERT J. GUERARD has published six novels (including *Night Journey, The Bystander* and *The Exiles*) and critical books on Robert Bridges, André Gide and Conrad. Formerly Professor of English at Harvard, he has been Professor of Literature at Stanford University since 1961.

ELOISE KNAPP HAY is a Lecturer in English at the University of California, Santa Barbara. She is the author of *The Political Novels of Joseph Conrad.*

ROBERT B. HEILMAN is Chairman of the Department of English at the University of Washington. His most recent work of literary criticism, *Tragedy and Melodrama: Versions of Experience,* will be published in the Fall of 1968.

DOUGLAS HEWITT is the author of *Conrad: A Reassessment.*

FREDERICK KARL is Professor of English at the City College of New York. He is the author of *The Contemporary English Novel* and co-editor of the *Collected Letters of Joseph Conrad,* to be published in 1972.

F. R. LEAVIS is the author of *The Great Tradition* and many other volumes of literary criticism. His most recent work is *Anna Karenina and Other Essays.*

TONY TANNER is a fellow of Queen's College, Cambridge and the author of many articles on modern literary figures.

DOROTHY VAN GHENT is the author of *The English Novel: Form and Function* and co-editor of *Continental Literature: An Anthology.*

PAUL L. WILEY is Professor of English at the University of Wisconsin. He is the author of *Conrad's Measure of Man; Novelist of Three Worlds: Ford Madox Ford;* and *English Poetry 1880 to 1920: The Edwardian Voice.*

MORTON DAUWEN ZABEL (1941–1964), critic and teacher, is the author of *Craft and Character in Modern Fiction* and editor of the Viking *Portable Conrad,* and the Riverside Edition of *Lord Jim.*

Selected Bibliography

Beebe, Maurice, "Criticism of Joseph Conrad: A Selected Checklist," *Modern Fiction Studies*, XI (Spring 1964), 81–106. (For more recent items, see the annual Bibliography of the *Publications of the Modern Language Association*.)

Ford, Ford Madox, *Joseph Conrad: A Personal Remembrance* (Boston, Mass.: Little, Brown and Company, 1924). An excellent early commentary on Conrad's techniques by Conrad's collaborator.

Gordon, John Dozier, *Joseph Conrad: The Making of a Novelist* (Cambridge, Mass.: Harvard University Press, 1940). An excellent study of the sources of Conrad's early fiction.

Guerard, Albert J., *Conrad The Novelist* (Cambridge, Mass.: Harvard University Press, 1965). An indispensable critical reading of Conrad's works. Chapters IV and V treat *Lord Jim*.

Hewitt, Douglas, *Conrad: A Reassessment* (Cambridge, England: Bowes & Bowes, 1952). A discriminating assessment of the major works. Chapter III deals with *Lord Jim*.

Jean-Aubry, G., *Joseph Conrad: Life and Letters*, 2 Vols. (New York: Doubleday & Company, Inc., 1927). This biography has been superseded by Baines' work, but the collection of letters is rich and varied.

Karl, Frederick, *A Reader's Guide to Joseph Conrad* (New York: Noonday Press, 1960). A useful introduction to Conrad's fiction. Pages 120–31 discuss *Lord Jim*.

Krieger, Murray, *The Tragic Vision: Variations on a Theme in Literary Interpretation* (New York: Holt, Rinehart & Winston, Inc., 1960). Pages 165–79 discuss *Lord Jim*.

Morf, Gustav, *The Polish Heritage of Joseph Conrad* (London: Sampson Low, Marston & Co., Ltd., 1929). A spirited but biased reading of Conrad's fiction in the light of his background.

Mudrick, Marvin, ed., *Conrad: A Collection of Critical Essays* (Englewood Cliffs, N.J.: Prentice-Hall, Inc., 1966). Essays by a dozen critics on many aspects of Conrad's art.

Sherry, Norman, *Conrad's Eastern World* (Cambridge, Mass.: Harvard University Press, 1966). The most recent and most detailed study of Conrad's Eastern sources.

Zabel, Morton Dauwen, *Craft and Character in Modern Fiction* (New York: The Viking Press, 1957). This volume includes four essays on Conrad by one of his most perceptive critics.

TWENTIETH CENTURY
INTERPRETATIONS

MAYNARD MACK, *Series Editor*
Yale University

NOW AVAILABLE
Collections of Critical Essays
ON